ALSO BY TED RALL

The Book of Obama: From Hope and Change to the Age of Revolt
The Anti-American Manifesto
The Year of Loving Dangerously (with Pablo G. Callejo)
America Gone Wild: Cartoons
Silk Road to Ruin: Is Central Asia the New Middle East?
Generalissimo el Busho: Essays and Cartoons on the Bush Years
Wake Up . . . You're Liberal! How We Can Take
  America Back from the Right
Gas War: The Truth Behind the American Occupation of Afghanistan
To Afghanistan and Back: A Graphic Travelogue
Search and Destroy: Cartoons
2024: A Graphic Novel
My War with Brian
Revenge of the Latchkey Kids: An Illustrated Guide to
  Surviving the 90s and Beyond
Real Americans Admit: "The Worst Thing I've Ever Done!"
All the Rules Have Changed: More Cartoons
Waking Up in America: Cartoons

AS EDITOR
Attitude: The New Subversive Political Cartoonists, volumes 1–3

AFTER WE KILL YOU, WE WILL WELCOME YOU BACK AS HONORED GUESTS

AFTER WE KILL YOU, WE WILL WELCOME YOU BACK AS HONORED GUESTS

UNEMBEDDED IN AFGHANISTAN

TED RALL

HILL AND WANG   A DIVISION OF FARRAR, STRAUS AND GIROUX   NEW YORK

Hill and Wang
A division of Farrar, Straus and Giroux
18 West 18th Street, New York 10011

Library of Congress Cataloging-in-Publication Data
Rall, Ted.
    After we kill you, we will welcome you back as honored guests : unembedded in
Afghanistan / Ted Rall.
        pages   cm
    ISBN 978-0-8090-2340-0 (hardback) — ISBN 978-1-4299-5558-4 (ebook)
    1. Afghan War, 2001——United States—Comic books, strips, etc.   2. Afghanistan—
Social conditions—21st century—Comic books, strips, etc.   3. Rall, Ted—Travel—
Afghanistan—Comic books, strips, etc.   4. Afghan War, 2001——United States—Blogs.
5. Afghanistan—Social conditions—21st century—Blogs.   6. Rall, Ted—Travel—
Afghanistan—Blogs.   7. Graphic novels.   I. Title.

DS371.412 .R35 2014
958.104'7—dc23

                                                                    2013038793

Designed by Abby Kagan

Hill and Wang books may be purchased for educational, business, or promotional use.
For information on bulk purchases, please contact the Macmillan Corporate and
Premium Sales Department at 1-800-221-7945, extension 5442, or write to
specialmarkets@macmillan.com.

www.fsgbooks.com
www.twitter.com/fsgbooks • www.facebook.com/fsgbooks

10   9   8   7   6   5   4   3   2   1

CONTENTS

AUTHOR'S NOTE

I t was the early eighties. The USSR had recently invaded Afghanistan, and the British journalist Robert Fisk was there to cover the occupation.

After he heard about fighting north of Kabul, Fisk asked the Soviet authorities for permission to travel to the battle zone. They refused. He went anyway.

Russian troops arrested him, put him in one of their vehicles, and headed back to Kabul. On the way the Soviets were ambushed by the mujahideen. The situation soon became desperate. A Soviet officer shoved a gun into Fisk's hands. Faced with a choice between journalistic objectivity and dying in a hail of bullets, Fisk did what anyone would do: he took the gun and started firing. It wasn't like the Afghans were asking to see press credentials.

In simpler times, we would say that Fisk had been morally compromised. In the parlance of twenty-first-century war correspondency, he had been "embedded."

Rolled out by the Pentagon for the 2003 invasion of Iraq, the "embedding" of American reporters into U.S. combat units in Iraq and Afghanistan has since become the standard way for print and broadcast reporters to cover wars.

"Independent" reporting—traveling on your own, relying on your wits and local contacts as you come across them—is now virtually unheard of. Mainly, this is because reporting from war zones is expensive.

Most war journalists are sponsored or employed by a major media organization; these outfits retain lawyers dedicated to limiting legal exposure. Attorneys think it's safer for reporters to travel as embeds.

They are mistaken. Not only does embedding make for terrible reporting, it is dangerous—not just for embeds, who come under fire at the same time as the soldiers with whom they travel and are widely perceived as shills for a brutal occupation, but for independents like me.

Here's how embedding works: before joining "their" battalions, reporters sign contracts agreeing to subject their dispatches to military censorship. They take a brief training class. Off they go.

About six hundred reporters covered Iraq as embeds in 2003. Journos on the scene guesstimated that only fifty to seventy saw anything interesting. Many were assigned to units that never deployed.

Ironically, independent reporters weren't brought in to fill up the slack. "One troubling side effect of the program was that it created a credentialing system among reporters: The embedded were considered official journalists, to whom the military would generally talk, and the 'unilaterals' were often treated as pests with no right to the battlefield," Jack Shafer wrote for *Slate* in May 2003. "In many instances, the military prevented unilaterals from covering the war."

The prevalence of embedding denies citizens of U.S.-occupied Iraq and Afghanistan chances to talk to American reporters. At most, the locals catch a fleeting glimpse of "reporters" buried in body armor, huddled with U.S. and NATO forces as they zoom past in troop convoys.

Editors, oblivious in climatized corporate offices, are happy.

"From what a blinding sandstorm feels like to reporting how one of our embeds broke his unit's coffee pot, we're giving readers a better sense of the field," Susan Stevenson of *The Atlanta Journal-Constitution* gushed as the Iraq War began. But the embeds can't show something more important: what U.S. occupation looks like to the people on the ground, the Iraqis and Afghans. Why are local people angry? American media consumers have no way to find out. They'll be shocked by the next 9/11.

I spent the late summer of 2010 traveling independently through Afghanistan with a pair of fellow cartoonists, Steven L. Cloud and Matt Bors. Odd birds who didn't fit into the embedded reporter narrative, we were repeatedly detained and questioned by Afghan national police who'd never encountered a "unilateral" reporter in ten years of war between the United States and the Taliban.

When we met Talibs and their sympathizers we had to talk fast in order to convince them that we weren't propaganda tools of the United States and the Karzai puppet government. Reporters are perceived as stooges because of the embedding program.

"Frankly, our job is to win the war," Marine Colonel Rick Long commented in 2003. "Part of that is information warfare. So we are going to attempt to dominate the information environment."

It's working.

"Just because the military ended up liking the embed program—General Tommy Franks told Fox News that he was 'a fan'—doesn't mean the program was bad," reasoned Shafer.

"There's nothing wrong with having respect in our hearts for the men and women who are fighting this war," added Bob Steele of the Poynter Institute.

My BS detector disagrees.

Reporters should strive for the impossible: objectivity. When covering a war it is not enough for them to be journalists first, Americans second. They should be journalists, pure and simple. Reporters can't even pretend to search for objective truth when they rely on "their" combat units to protect them, provide them with access to stories, and transmit those stories to their organizations.

Under the embedding regime, the war reporting we get in U.S. newspapers and broadcast outlets obsesses over the experience of American soldiers. Meanwhile, the accounts of civilians and "enemy" fighters go untold. The Taliban are right when they say that American war journalism has been reduced to rank propaganda.

A 2006 Penn State study looked at seven hundred forty-two print news stories filed from Iraq during the 2003 invasion for sixty-seven outlets, including *The New York Times*, *The Washington Post*, the *Los Angeles Times*, *USA Today*, the *Chicago Tribune*, Reuters, and the Associated Press. Researchers found that 93 percent of stories filed by embedded reporters relied on U.S. soldiers as their primary source. The number was 43 percent for independent reporters.

Conversely, independent reporters were much more likely to cover Iraqi civilians: 73 percent versus 43 percent.

Not surprisingly, newspaper editors preferred the stories about American troops. Which is why the vast majority—seventy-one percent of stories that appeared in print—were written by embeds.

"The majority of war coverage in the study heavily emphasized the soldiers' experiences of the war while downplaying the effects of the invasion on the Iraqi people," said Andrew Lindner, a graduate student in sociology at Penn State.

Any media organization worthy of the name should pull its reporters out of the embedding program.

By the Way

Throughout this work I refer to the involvement of U.S. military forces in Afghanistan as "the war against Afghanistan." Like all choices of language, this is a political choice.

Most daily newspapers and national news broadcasts call it "the war in Afghanistan." I reject the preposition as excessively bland. It is true that there is a war *in* Afghanistan (though one undeclared by any legal authority), but "in" glosses over the fact of U.S. involvement—involvement, hell, it was an invasion. Indeed, there would probably not be a war there at all if not for the United States. When the war began in October 2001, the Taliban controlled 95 percent of the country. Their principal adversary in the civil conflict of the 1990s, the Northern Alliance, were reduced to the sparsely populated mountain redoubt of Badakhshan, the remote buffer strip in the northeast that separates the former USSR from ex–British India. The Alliance were all but finished. They would have been overrun in a year or two had the United States not gone in.

It's our war. We ought to say so.

One could fairly speak of the American *occupation* of Afghanistan. Indeed, I did so in the subtitle of my 2003 book about the benighted Trans-Afghanistan Pipeline project. However, it has since become clear that neither the United States nor its NATO allies intend to impose the high-density distribution of troops and civilian personnel characteristic of an occupation. So that doesn't work either.

Given what followed the fall 2001 invasion, "Operation Enduring Freedom" is an absurdly cynical misnomer at best. The American machinations that led to the installation of Hamid Karzai, a puppet exile mostly devoid of indigenous support, not to mention "elections" in which more Afghans voted than the country's population, make any association with the word "freedom" a joke.

Although imperfect, I use "the war against Afghanistan" because it makes the point. It speaks to the war's effect. The invasion and ensuing pseudo-occupation has ravaged the Afghan people. As you will read ahead, the war has led to significant infrastructure reconstruction. But the overall effect has been devastating. Tens of thousands, probably hundreds of thousands, of Afghans have died. Most of the country has become more lawless than ever. Worst of all, it has demoralized the Afghans, a proud and indomitable people.

Fortunately, in the war against Afghanistan, the Afghans will prevail.

They always do.

HISTORY OF THE U.S. WAR IN AFGHANISTAN

Dispensing with the usual recap of the Soviet occupation of the 1980s, which is well documented, BUT including the largely unknown (or, more accurately, unnoticed) pre-history leading up to the 2001 invasion and continuing from there to the present ongoing despair

ON SEPTEMBER 11, 2001, FOUR PASSENGER JETS WERE HIJACKED. THREE WERE FLOWN INTO BUILDINGS. ONE CRASHED IN A FIELD IN WESTERN PENNSYLVANIA.

WAR AGAINST AFGHANISTAN FOLLOWED LESS THAN A MONTH LATER.

BUT WAR WAS NOT A FOREGONE CONCLUSION.

Kabul

NOT AGAINST
AFGHANISTAN, ANYWAY.

15 OF THE HIJACKERS WERE FROM SAUDI ARABIA, 2 FROM THE U.A.E., 1 FROM EGYPT, 1 FROM LEBANON.

TRUE, SOME OF THEM HAD ATTENDED JIHADI TRAINING CAMPS IN AFGHANISTAN.

NO ONE THOUGHT THE TALIBAN HAD PLANNED OR ORDERED THE ATTACKS.

Mullah Omar

Supreme Leader— Taliban

BEFORE 9/11, THE U.S.' RELATIONSHIP WITH THE TALIBAN WAS CHARACTERIZED BY, DEPENDING ON YOUR PERSPECTIVE, NUANCE OR HYPOCRITICAL CONTRADICTION AT THE HIGHEST LEVELS.

IT'S LIKE **TAIWAN**. WE GUARANTEE WE WON'T LET THEM BE INVADED BY **CHINA**. BUT WE ONLY HAVE FULL DIPLOMATIC RELATIONS WITH CHINA.

BURHANUDDIN RABBANI OF THE ISLAMIC STATE OF AFGHANISTAN, ALSO CALLED THE UNITED FRONT, UNOFFICIALLY KNOWN AS THE NORTHERN ALLIANCE, WAS THE INTERNATIONALLY RECOGNIZED PRESIDENT OF AFGHANISTAN FROM 1996 TO 2001.

Flag of the Islamic State of Afghanistan

THE ALLIANCE HELD AFGHANISTAN'S SEAT AT THE U.N. AND ALMOST ALL OF THE NATION'S EMBASSIES AROUND THE WORLD.

WHAT HELP HAS THE U.S. GIVEN YOU?

ONCE THEY SENT US THIS MAP OF AFGHANISTAN. BUT THE SOVIET ONES ARE MORE UP-TO-DATE

U.S. AFGHAN AMBASSADOR TO UZBEKISTAN

1999

BUT REALITY ON THE GROUND WAS VERY DIFFERENT. TALIBAN FORCES, BACKED BY PAKISTANI INTELLIGENCE (WHICH WAS IN TURN FINANCED AND TRAINED BY THE AMERICAN CIA), HAD PUSHED RABBANI AND HIS MAIN WARLORD, AHMED SHAH MASSOUD, INTO THE NORTHEASTERN CORNER OF THE COUNTRY.

UZBEKISTAN

Dushanbe

KYRGYZSTAN

CHINA

CIA Director George Tenet

AFGHANISTAN

Kabul

IRAN

Islamabad

Pervez Musharraf

PAKISTAN

dictator of Pakistan

NEPAL

Mullah Omar

Taliban leader

Taliban-controlled

Northern Alliance-controlled

BY 2001 THE NORTHERN ALLIANCE CONTROLLED LESS THAN 10% OF THE COUNTRY. TRAPPED IN THEIR REDOUBT IN THE HIGH-ALTITUDE PROVINCE OF BADAKHSHAN, ANALYSTS PREDICTED THEY WOULD BE SLAUGHTERED IN THEIR "CAPITAL," FAIZABAD, OR FORCED TO RETREAT INTO TAJIKISTAN BY 2002.

THE TALIBAN ENJOYED FORMAL RECOGNITION FROM A PALTRY 3 NATIONS: PAKISTAN, SAUDI ARABIA, AND THE UNITED ARAB EMIRATES.

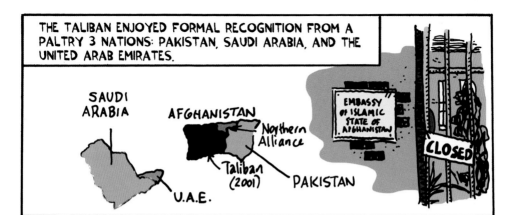

DIPLOMATIC FICTIONS ASIDE, THE U.S. HAD EXTENSIVE DEALINGS WITH THE TALIBAN BEFORE 9/11.

MAINLY, THEY THREATENED TO STARVE THEM.

THE TRADE SANCTIONS ARE HURTING OUR PEOPLE—

MAYBE WE'LL START **NEW ONES**

MORE OFTEN, HOWEVER, THEY SUCKED UP TO THEM.

THERE IS THE THEORETICAL POLITICAL SITUATION: YOU ARE DIPLOMATICALLY ISOLATED. THE U.N. SEAT BELONGS TO THE NORTHERN ALLIANCE.

ON THE OTHER HAND, THERE IS REALITY ON THE GROUND. YOU CONTROL MOST OF THE COUNTRY. THE CIVIL WAR'S MOMENTUM FAVORS YOU. AND THERE ARE CERTAIN **STRATEGIC CONSIDERATIONS.**

THE CLINTON ADMINISTRATION TALKED TO TALIBAN OFFICIALS ABOUT THE TRANS-AFGHANISTAN PIPELINE, A PLAN BACKED BY UNION OIL OF CALIFORNIA (UNOCAL) TO CARRY OIL AND NATURAL GAS FROM KAZAKHSTAN AND TURKMENISTAN FROM HERAT TO KANDAHAR TO A DEEP-SEA PORT ON THE ARABIAN SEA IN PAKISTAN.

TALIBAN LEADERS FLEW TO UNOCAL'S HEADQUARTERS IN SUGARLAND, TEXAS, IN DECEMBER 1997. THE TALKS WENT NOWHERE BECAUSE THE TWO SIDES COULDN'T AGREE ON TRANSIT FEES.

RELATIONS COOLED AFTER OSAMA BIN LADEN CLAIMED RESPONSIBILITY FOR BOMBING OF U.S. EMBASSIES IN EAST AFRICA IN 1998.

@*#! FREEZE 'EM OUT. EVERYTHING IS ON HOLD UNTIL FURTHER NOTICE.

GEORGE W. BUSH, A FORMER TEXAS OIL MAN WHOSE ADVISORS HAD CLOSE TIES TO THE ENERGY BUSINESS, BECAME PRESIDENT IN JANUARY 2001.

Referring to the disputed 2000 election, I drew him as "Generalissimo El Busho"

Coke Snot

IN FEBRUARY 2001 BUSH'S NEW ADMINISTRATION AGREED TO FUNNEL $43 MILLION THROUGH THE U.N. TO THE TALIBAN REGIME, OSTENSIBLY TO FINANCE A BAN ON CULTIVATION OF AFGHAN OPIUM POPPIES, THE SOURCE OF 90% OF ALL THE HEROIN ON EARTH. THE TALIBAN USED THE MONEY, RECEIVED IN MAY, TO PAY GOVERNMENT SALARIES.

THOUGH BRUTAL, THE JOINT U.S.-TALIBAN DRUG INTERDICTION PROGRAM WAS SUCCESSFUL.

MEANWHILE, THE WHITE HOUSE CONTACTED THE TALIBAN TO REOPEN NEGOTIATIONS FOR THE STALLED TRANS-AFGHANISTAN PIPELINE PROJECT.

IN MARCH, PERHAPS IN PART AS A BARGAINING TACTIC, THE TALIBAN BLEW UP A PAIR OF FAMOUS 6TH CENTURY BUDDHA STATUES AT BAMIYAN.

THAT SUMMER, THE TALKS BROKE DOWN. AGAIN, THE STICKING POINT WAS TRANSIT FEES.

THE TALIBAN MET U.S. OFFICIALS AT LEAST 20 TIMES BETWEEN 1998 AND 2001 TO DISCUSS THE OIL AND GAS PIPELINE, COUNTERNARCOTICS, AND AMERICAN REQUESTS TO EXTRADITE OSAMA BIN LADEN.

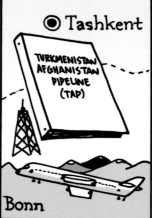

A FLURRY OF MEETINGS TOOK PLACE IN TASHKENT, UZBEKISTAN; KANDAHAR, AFGHANISTAN; ISLAMABAD, PAKISTAN; BONN, GERMANY; AND NEW YORK CITY.

THERE WERE SATELLITE CALLS, ONE OF WHICH INVOLVED A 40-MINUTE CHAT BETWEEN A MID-LEVEL STATE DEPARTMENT BUREAUCRAT AND THE TALIBAN'S SUPREME LEADER, MOHAMMED OMAR.

GEORGE W. BUSH EVEN COLLECTED A GIFT, A HANDSOME CARPET, FROM RAHMATULLAH HASHEMI, THE PERSONAL ENVOY OF TALIBAN SUPREME LEADER MULLAH OMAR, WHO FLEW TO A PIPELINE CHAT IN WASHINGTON IN MARCH 2001.

THEN: 9/11.

THE HIJACKERS WERE MOSTLY FROM SAUDI ARABIA. BUT THERE WAS NO TALK OF WAR, OR EVEN ECONOMIC SANCTIONS, AGAINST THE KINGDOM.

THE SAUDIS FINANCE THE RADICAL MADRASSAS. THEY SPREAD RADICAL WAHHABISM. THEY **ARE** RADICAL ISLAM.

BUT THEY HAVE THE MOST OIL.

NEVER MIND.

THEY HAD TRAINED AT CAMPS FINANCED BY—AND MOSTLY IN—PAKISTAN, WHICH ALSO WAS ONE OF THE LEADING EXPORTERS OF ANTI-AMERICAN JIHADISM IN THE WORLD. DESPITE ITS INVOLVEMENT, THERE WOULD BE NO ATTACK AGAINST PAKISTAN.

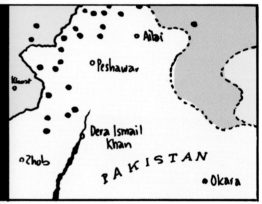

INSTEAD, THE U.S. BEGAN POURING IN ADDITIONAL AID TO THE MILITARY DICTATORSHIP OF GENERAL PERVEZ MUSHARRAF. AS OF THIS WRITING, PAKISTAN'S GOVERNMENT HAS RECEIVED $26 BILLION IN MILITARY AND ECONOMIC FUNDING SINCE THE 9/11 TERRORIST ATTACKS.

AFGHANISTAN'S ROLE IN 9/11 HAD BEEN PERIPHERAL. NONETHELESS, AFGHANISTAN BECAME THE TARGET OF WHAT WOULD BECOME AMERICA'S LONGEST WAR.

BUT AFGHANISTAN DOESN'T HAVE ANY **TARGETS**. IT'S THE 14TH CENTURY THERE.

BUT IT'S EASY.

BIN LADEN EXPRESSLY DENIED BEING INVOLVED.

I WOULD LIKE TO ASSURE THE WORLD THAT I DID NOT PLAN THE RECENT ATTACKS, WHICH SEEM TO HAVE BEEN PLANNED BY PEOPLE FOR PERSONAL REASONS.

Sept. 15, 2001

NONETHELESS, AFTER 9/11, THE BUSH ADMINISTRATION ISSUED A DEMAND THAT THE TALIBAN TURN OVER BIN LADEN.

NO QUESTION HE IS THE PRIME SUSPECT. NO QUESTION ABOUT THAT.

Sept. 16, 2001

ALTHOUGH THE TWO GOVERNMENTS DIDN'T HAVE AN EXTRADICTION TREATY, THE TALIBAN OFFERED TO COMPLY IN EXCHANGE FOR EVIDENCE OF BIN LADEN'S COMPLICITY IN THE 9/11 ATTACKS.

WE KNOW HE'S GUILTY. TURN HIM OVER. THERE'S NO NEED TO DISCUSS INNOCENCE OR GUILT.

Bush Rejec
Offer to Su

By Kathy Gannon
Associated Press Writer
Sunday, October 14, 2001

JALALABAD, Afghanistan—A se
Taliban leader said Sunday that th
Islamic militia would be willing to ha
over Osama bin Laden to a third country
if the United States halts the bomb

BUSH REJECTED THEIR OFFER.

LOOKING BACK, IT'S HARD TO SEE WHAT THE TALIBAN COULD HAVE DONE TO AVOID THE INVASION.

IT'S MORE THAN POSSIBLE THAT THE TALIBAN WERE BLUFFING—THAT THEY COULDN'T TURN OVER BIN LADEN BECAUSE THEY DIDN'T KNOW WHERE HE WAS.

BUT THE SHEIKH IS IN A PAKISTANI MILITARY HOSPITAL IN ISLAMABAD—

SHUT UP.

SOME SOURCES SAY HE FLED TO PAKISTAN AFTER THE KILLING OF SHAH MASSOUD ON 9-9-01. IN THIS SCENARIO, HE WAS OUT OF THE COUNTRY ON 9/11.

ACCORDING TO OTHER ACCOUNTS, HE WENT TO THE 1980s-ERA TUNNELS IN THE TORA BORA MOUNTAINS.

THOUGH CORNERED, HE SOMEHOW MANAGED TO ESCAPE THE CAVE COMPLEX.

THE MAIN REASON GIVEN TO INVADE AFGHANISTAN—CAPTURING OSAMA BIN LADEN TO BRING HIM TO JUSTICE—COULDN'T BE TRUE.

"CBS News has been told that the night before the September 11 terrorist attack, Osama bin Laden was in Pakistan."

—Barry Petersen
CBS News, Jan. 28, 2002

THE AL QAEDA LEADER WAS IN PAKISTAN ALL ALONG. AND THE U.S. KNEW THAT ALL ALONG.

JUMP AHEAD TO 2011, WHEN U.S. COMMANDOS CAUGHT UP WITH BIN LADEN IN ABBOTTABAD, AN UPSCALE PAKISTANI SUBURB. NOT ONLY DID THEY MAKE NO EFFORT TO CAPTURE HIM ALIVE, THEY HELD HIM FOR A FEW MINUTES— THEN SHOT HIM. WHY DIDN'T THE U.S. WANT A TRIAL? MAYBE THEY DIDN'T WANT THESE FACTS OUT.

AS OF 9/11 THERE WERE ONLY 2 MILITANT TRAINING CAMPS IN OPERATION IN AFGHANISTAN. BOTH WERE PRIMARILY DEDICATED TO TRAINING TALIBAN RECRUITS. DOZENS OF CAMPS CONTINUED TO CHURN OUT TRAINED ISLAMIC RADICALS AFTER 2001. THESE WERE IN PAKISTAN, WHILE IT WAS RECEIVING HUNDREDS OF MILLIONS OF DOLLARS IN MILITARY FUNDING FROM THE U.S.

"Osama bin Laden was captured alive by US forces but shot him dead in front of family members, according to his daughter."
—*The Daily Telegraph,* May 4, 2011

THEN THERE WERE THE TRAINING CAMPS.

Al Farouq Camp near Kandahar, Afgh.

IF CLOSING THE CAMPS HAD BEEN A MAJOR OBJECTIVE OF THE WAR, THE U.S. WOULD HAVE INVADED PAKISTAN INSTEAD.

THE U.S. MILITARY CAMPAIGN AGAINST AFGHANISTAN UNFOLDED IN DISCRETE STAGES.

FIRST, ABOUT 800 U.S. SPECIAL FORCES TROOPS PARACHUTED INTO NORTHERN AFGHANISTAN.

SOME WERE ACCOMPANIED BY CIA OFFICERS CARRYING BRICKS OF $100 BILLS. THESE WERE USED TO BUY THE SUPPORT OF LOCAL WARLORDS AND COMMANDERS.

AND THERE'S MORE IF **YOU STAY BOUGHT.**

SPECIAL FORCES DIRECTED LASER-GUIDED "SMART BOMBS" AGAINST TALIBAN POSITIONS.

LOCK IN ON THESE COORDINATES:

THESE, ALONG WITH VIETNAM-ERA "CARPET BOMBING" FROM B-52S, ALLOWED THE NORTHERN ALLIANCE TO ADVANCE.

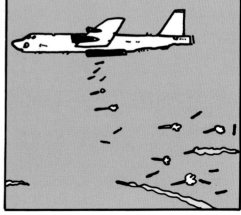

BY 2009 THE U.S. HAD DROPPED MORE THA[N] [ ],000 TONS OF BOMBS, INCLUDING CLUSTER BOMBS PAI[N]D BRIGHT COLORS TO A[TT]RACT CHILDREN AND "DAISY C[U]TTER" BOMBS THAT USE DEPLETED UR[A]NIUM.

◉ Kabul

KABUL, CONSIDERED ENEMY TERRITORY BY THE KANDAHAR-BASED TALIBAN, FELL IN NOVEMBER 2001.

NEXT THE TALIBAN LOST [IT]S SOUTHERN STRONGHOLD. MOHAMMED OMAR AND OTHER LEADERS FLED THE BOMBARDMENT BY HORSE AND DIRTBIKE.

THE BATTLE OF KUNDUZ, MARKED BY TREACHERY AND A LEVEL OF BRUTALITY HIGH EVEN BY AFGHAN STANDARDS, WAS THE LAST STAND OF THE OLD TALIBAN.

PAKISTAN'S ISI INTELLIGENCE AGENCY AND THE CIA COORDINATED A SERIES OF FLIGHTS FOR FOREIGN "ARABI" FIGHTERS OUT OF KUNDUZ TO PAKISTAN.

THEY WOULD HAVE BEEN KILLED HAD THEY STAYED.

AFTER THE EVACUATION, REMAINING TALIBAN COMMANDERS RADIOED THEIR NORTHERN ALLIANCE COUNTERPARTS TO ARRANGE SURRENDER.

WE WANT TO DISCUSS TERMS.

BUT WHEN THE NORTHERN ALLIANCE SOLDIERS APPROACHED, THEY WERE AMBUSHED WITH A HAIL OF GUNFIRE.

FURIOUS AT THIS ACT OF BETRAYAL, NORTHERN ALLIANCE FORCES ACCOMPANIED BY U.S. SPECIAL FORCES FOUGHT THEIR WAY INTO KUNDUZ. THERE THEY SEIZED AT LEAST 7500 PRISONERS, INCLUDING CHECHENS, UZBEKS, AND PAKISTANIS WHO DIDN'T CATCH PLANES OUT.

AMONG THEM WAS JOHNNY WALKER LINDH, THE "AMERICAN TALIBAN" NOW SERVING 19 YEARS IN FEDERAL PRISON ON WEAPONS CHARGES.

MOST OF THE TALIBS WERE LOCKED IN SHIPPING CONTAINERS AND SHIPPED TO THE DESERT AT DASHT-I-LEILI, WHERE THEY WERE MASSACRED AND DUMPED IN A MASS GRAVE.

"At the time they were taking prisoners from Qaala Zeini to Scheberghan. I went to fill my car with petrol. I smelled something strange and asked the petrol attendant where the smell was coming from. He said 'look behind you,' and there were trucks with containers fixed on them. I was surprised. I saw something very strange. Blood was leaking from the containers—they were full of dead bodies."

—Afghan taxi driver in the documentary film *Afghan Massacre* (2002)

Bakawal Khorasan
to
Sheberghan

Dasht-i-Leili

Pits

Dasht-i-Leili
Desert

AFGHANISTAN

Notorious Uzbek warlord Rashid Dostum, accused of ordering the massacre

In 2009, U.S. President Obama promised to look into Dasht-i-Leili. He never did.

THERE ARE SUBSTANTIATED REPORTS THAT U.S. SPECIAL FORCES WITNESSED THE SLAUGHTER.

EXPERTS EXPECTED THAT THE DEPOSED KING MOHAMMED ZAHIR SHAH, 87 AND LIVING IN EXILE IN ITALY, WOULD FORM A TRANSITIONAL UNITY GOVERNMENT AFTER THE FALL OF THE TALIBAN.

BEHIND THE SCENES, HOWEVER, THE U.S. PUSHED ITS MAN, HAMID KARZAI, AT THE *LOYA JIRGA*. THE KING WAS SHUNTED ASIDE AND SOON FORGOTTEN.

DAYS BEFORE THE END OF 2001, KARZAI ASSUMED THE CHAIRMANSHIP OF A TRANSITIONAL GOVERNING COUNCIL.

KARZAI, SINCE DERIDED AS THE "MAYOR OF KABUL" BECAUSE HIS GOVERNMENT'S POWER NEVER EXTENDS MUCH BEYOND THE CAPITAL, HAS SINCE BEEN THE DE FACTO PUPPET PRESIDENT-FOR-LIFE OF U.S.-OCCUPIED AFGHANISTAN.

AT THIS WRITING, HE HAS NOT BEEN ASSASSINATED.

THE OCCUPATION OF AFGHANISTAN FORMALLY BEGAN IN 2002, WHEN THE U.S. FORMED THE INTERNATIONAL SECURITY ASSISTANCE FORCE (ISAF) UNDER U.N. AUSPICES. ISAF CURRENTLY COMPRISES ALLIED OCCUPATION SOLDIERS FROM 45 COUNTRIES, HALF OF THEM AMERICAN.

ISAF'S MISSION WAS OSTENSIBLY TO PROVIDE SECURITY, TRAIN THE KARZAI REGIME'S POLICE AND MILITARY, THUS ALLOWING INTERNATIONAL AID ORGANIZATIONS AND U.S. GOVERNMENT AGENCIES TO BEGIN REBUILDING THE NATION, WHICH HAD BEEN REDUCED TO RUBBLE DURING MORE THAN TWO DECADES OF CIVIL WAR.

IN REALITY, ISAF SPENT MOST OF ITS TIME, MONEY, AND ENERGY BATTLING THE NEO-TALIBAN.* THE KARZAI REGIME WAS DEEMED TOO CORRUPT TO BE GIVEN CONTROL OVER RECONSTRUCTION FUNDS, AID AGENCIES SPENT DONOR CASH ON EXTRAVAGANT LIVING, AND SECURITY WAS NONEXISTENT.

The Agency Coordinating Body for Afghan Relief (ACBAR) office rented a house in Kabul for an extravagant $13,000 a month in 2002.

NGOs tool around in white Land Rovers

* MORE ON THE NEO-TALIBAN LATER

AS LATE AS 2005, NOT A SINGLE INCH OF ROADWAY OR A SINGLE BUILDING HAD BEEN BUILT BY THE U.S. NEVERTHELESS, BILLIONS OF DOLLARS HAD BEEN SPENT THERE—WHERE AND ON WHAT, NO ONE WOULD SAY.

Aid promised to Afghanistan by international community at the 2003 Tokyo conference:
$4.5 billion
—1.5 billion to the UN
—1.5 billion to NGOs
 1.5 billion net

\# NGOs deemed to have given zero aid to Afghans: 80%

ALL THAT CHANGED WAS THE NATURE OF THE CIVIL WAR. IT WAS NO LONGER THE TALIBAN VS. THE NORTHERN ALLIANCE. NOW IT WAS THE NEO-TALIBAN VS. THE U.S., ITS ALLIES, AND THE NORTHERN ALLIANCE-DOMINATED GOVERNMENT.

DURING THE EARLY YEARS, MOST OF THE FIGHTING OCCURRED IN TALIBAN STRONGHOLDS IN THE MOUNTAINS OF EASTERN AFGHANISTAN, ALONG THE PAKISTANI BORDER.

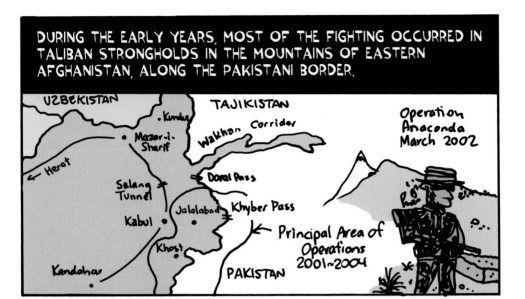

BY 2005 AND 2006 THE FRONTS HAD EXPANDED TO THE SOUTH, ESPECIALLY IN THE POPPY FIELDS OF HELMAND PROVINCE, AND THE REMOTE WESTERN DESERTS BORDERING IRAN.

ISAF ESTABLISHED PROVINCIAL RECONSTRUCTION TEAMS (PRTs) THROUGHOUT THE COUNTRYSIDE. ISAF WORKS WITH LOCAL AFGHANS, TRIES TO EARN HEARTS AND MINDS WITH REBUILDING PROJECTS, BUT THE NEO-TALIBAN STYMIE THEM.

I ASKED REPRESENTATIVES OF THE LITHUANIAN-LED PRT IN GHOR PROVINCE WHAT THEY HAD ACCOMPLISHED IN FIVE YEARS. THEY POINTED TO A HALF-KILOMETER STRETCH OF FRESHLY PAVED ASPHALT.

THIS IS IT?

UH-HUH

LIKE THE BRITISH AND THE SOVIETS, AMERICAN FORCES RARELY INTERACTED WITH THE LOCAL POPULATION, EXCEPT TO DRIVE AROUND SHOOTING THEM. AT BAGRAM AIRBASE, A FORMER SOVIET FACILITY NORTH OF KABUL, TENS OF THOUSANDS OF ISAF FORCES SETTLED INTO A DE FACTO "GREEN ZONE" WITH ITS OWN ATMS, BURGER KING, STARBUCKS, AND SIGNS REFERENCING HOW THIS WAS ABOUT GETTING EVEN FOR 9/11.

HIDING INSIDE MILITARY BASES DIDN'T WORK EITHER. AFGHANISTAN BECAME SO DANGEROUS THAT, BY 2007, A U.S. SOLDIER STATIONED THERE WAS MORE LIKELY TO GET KILLED OR WOUNDED THAN IN IRAQ.

BY 2008 THE OCCUPATION OF AFGHANISTAN, ORIGINALLY DUBBED "THE GOOD WAR" (AS OPPOSED TO THE WAR OF CHOICE AGAINST IRAQ) BY LIBERAL MEDIA, HAD PLUNGED IN POPULARITY IN OPINION POLLS.

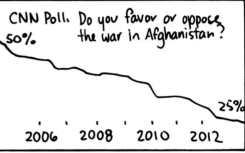

SEASONED CENTRAL ASIA ANALYSTS BEGAN SPEAKING ABOUT THE RISE OF THE "NEO-TALIBAN." UNLIKE THE ASCETICS LED BY MULLAH OMAR AND VETERANS OF THE ANTI-SOVIET JIHAD— THEY WERE FANATICS, BUT THEY WERE CERTAINLY NOT CORRUPT— THE YOUNGER GENERATION OF SELF-DESCRIBED "TALIBAN" WAS RAISED IN SAUDI-FUNDED MADRASSAS IN PAKISTANI REFUGEE CAMPS. CYNICS WHO VICTIMIZED DEVOUT MUSLIMS, THEY USED RADICAL ISLAM AS A COVER FOR CRIMINAL ENTERPRISES RANGING FROM OPIUM TRAFFICKING TO KIDNAPPING.

DURING THE 2008 U.S. PRESIDENTIAL CAMPAIGN, OBAMA REPEATEDLY ATTACKED BUSH AND THE REPUBLICANS ON FOREIGN POLICY AND WAR, TRADITIONALLY THEIR GREATEST STRENGTH. HE ARGUED THAT AFGHANISTAN, "THE GOOD WAR," HAD GONE WRONG BECAUSE TROOPS AND FUNDING HAD BEEN TRANSFERRED TO THE WAR IN IRAQ.

WE TOOK OUR EYE OFF THE BALL WHEN WE INVADED IRAQ... OUR REAL FOCUS HAS TO BE ON AFGHANISTAN, THE BORDER REGIONS BETWEEN PAKISTAN AND AFGHANISTAN.

to Katie Couric

Jan. 14, 2009

AFTER THE ELECTION, OBAMA MADE GOOD ON HIS PROMISE, ORDERING AN ADDITIONAL 33,000 TROOPS IN A TEMPORARY "SURGE" MEANT TO BREAK THE NEO-TALIBAN SO THAT KARZAI'S AFGHAN NATIONAL ARMY WOULD BE ABLE TO "STEP UP," IN MILITARY JARGON, AFTER SCHEDULED WITHDRAWAL IN 2014.

BUT THE WAR WAS ALREADY LOST. GEN. STANLEY MCCHRYSTAL, OBAMA'S COMMANDER IN AFGHANISTAN, ANNOUNCED THAT THE TALIBAN HAD GAINED THE UPPER HAND.

THIS IS A PERIOD WHERE PEOPLE ARE REALLY LOOKING TO SEE WHICH WAY THIS IS GOING TO GO. IT'S THE CRITICAL AND DECISIVE MOMENT.

Aug. 10, '09

2010, THE YEAR OF THE SURGE, SAW HEAVY FIGHTING IN HELMAND AND KANDAHAR PROVINCES, AS WELL AS THE EAST, BUT VICTORIES WERE TEMPORARY. WORST OF ALL, THEY WERE OVERSHADOWED BY PARLIAMENTARY ELECTIONS TARNISHED BY TAMPERING AND CORRUPTION, THE COLLAPSE OF KABUL BANK, WHICH HAD BEEN LOOTED BY KARZAI'S FAMILY, AND THE WIKILEAKS DATA DUMP.

WIKILEAKS DOCUMENTS SHOWED THAT CIVILIAN CASUALTIES HAD BEEN EXTENSIVE, THE AFGHAN ARMY WAS USELESS, AND PAKISTAN'S ISI WAS SUPPORTING THE NEO-TALIBAN USING U.S. TAXPAYER MONEY.

AS THE BULK OF U.S. OCCUPATION TROOPS PREPARE TO LEAVE AFGHANISTAN, IT IS BECOMING CLEAR THAT MANY OF THE ORIGINAL WAR AIMS—THE PIPELINE, ESTABLISHING SECURITY, COUNTERNARCOTICS, DENYING A BASE TO RADICAL ISLAMISTS—HAVE BEEN ABANDONED. FROM A MILITARY STANDPOINT, AFGHANISTAN HAS BEEN REDUCED TO A STAGING AND LAUNCHING AREA FOR FIGHTER AND DRONE PLANE ATTACKS AGAINST THE TRIBAL AREAS OF PAKISTAN.

THEIR DRONES ARE EVERYWHERE. THEY CAN SEE EVERYTHING. WHY DON'T THEY USE THEIR DRONES TO KILL THE BANDITS WHO ROB US ON THE HIGHWAYS?

IRONICALLY, NATO FORCES HAVE MANAGED TO ADDRESS SOME OF THE COMPLAINTS THEY HEARD FROM 2001 TO 2005. MAIN HIGHWAYS, ESPECIALLY THE "RING ROAD" THAT CONNECTS MAJOR CITIES, HAVE BEEN PAVED. SOME SCHOOLS HAVE BEEN BUILT.

FOR AFGHANS, THOUGH, THESE IMPROVEMENTS WERE TOO FEW AND CAME TOO LATE. NOW THEIR CENTRAL CONCERN IS "SECURITY"— LAW AND ORDER. FROM THEIR STANDPOINT—AND IT IS HARD TO DISAGREE WITH THEM—U.S. AND NATO FORCES ARE CONCERNED WITH THEIR OWN SECURITY, OFTEN AT THE EXPENSE OF AFGHAN CIVILIANS.

BUT NOW YOU HAVE, FOR EXAMPLE, CELLPHONES.

WHICH THE BANDITS USE TO CALL IN RANSOM DEMANDS FOR THEIR KIDNAP VICTIMS.

WHATEVER FAITH THE POPULATION HAD IN KARZAI EVAPORATED WITH THE ANNOUCEMENT OF WITHDRAWAL IN 2014.

KARZAI? THIEF. SHOULD BE KILLED.

THE AMERICANS RAN UP AGAINST A SET OF UNSURMOUNTABLE OBSTACLES. FIRST, THEIR IGNORANCE OF AND REFUSAL TO ADAPT TO AFGHAN CULTURE.

OUT OF THE CAR!!

SECOND, A FRACTIOUS PEOPLE'S HISTORICAL WILLINGNESS TO UNITE TO FIGHT OFF INVADERS AFTER THEY HAVE SETTLED IN.

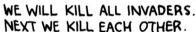

WE WILL KILL ALL INVADERS. NEXT WE KILL EACH OTHER.

AND THIRD, THE FACT THAT NO COUNTRY HAS SUCCESSFULLY OCCUPIED ANOTHER SINCE 1900.

IN MAY 2012, THE U.S. SIGNED A "STRATEGIC PARTNERSHIP AGREEMENT" WITH AFGHANISTAN, EFFECTIVE THROUGH 2024.

AFGHANISTAN'S WARLORDS ARE GEARING UP FOR ANOTHER FULL-FLEDGED CIVIL WAR. IN LATE 2011 ABDUL RASHID DOSTUM AND OTHERS REFORMED THE NORTHERN ALLIANCE TO FIGHT THE TALIBAN.

AFTER WE KILL YOU,
WE WILL WELCOME
YOU BACK AS
HONORED GUESTS

PROLOGUE: THE END OF THE BEGINNING

Afghanistan in 2001: there was nothing.

There were forty-five of us reporters. Eight Americans. Three in our car. We had no idea what we were in for.

Which is why we came. To see things for ourselves.

Not to get the truth. You can't get the truth.

But you can get an impression.

We huddled inside my fixer Sadoullo's car, furiously rubbing our legs, futilely trying to warm up. In late afternoon, when we'd arrived at the border crossing, it must have been in the high fifties or low sixties. It was nine o'clock now and well below freezing, and the breath of my wife and my agent and Sadoullo's driver and my own was all that was keeping us warm, spreading frost up the cracks on the windshield of Sadoullo's Volga, a conveyance that couldn't have been more poorly insulated had it been made of Saran Wrap. Time crawled. There was no telling how long the Russian guards would make us wait.

I got out of the car, found my backpack, and pulled out a string of silk underwear through a hole in the seam. Icy sand crunched beneath my boots. I found a spot behind a shipping container to pee and change. It wasn't colder outside than in the car.

I watched the guard shack as I shuffled out of my jeans. Along with smoke, tinny Russian disco and singing wafted out the flue and through coils of concertina wire. Drunken singing. The men of the Russian Army's 201st Motorized Rifle Division weren't going to skip their liquid dinner to cater to a convoy of trucks and jeeps carrying a bunch of self-important reporters who wanted to cross the Tajik-Afghan border. There was no rush. Afghanistan had been blowing itself up forever. As far as the Russians were concerned, we could just as easily get ourselves killed tomorrow.

A Soviet flag, crisp and bright and nowhere near ten years old, waved above an unmanned watchtower. You'd think the hammer and sickle would look incongruous, what with the country it symbolized having ceased to exist ten years earlier. But here, at the ass end of the world, things that didn't make sense were run of the mill. It was the twenty-first century. Yet the Tajik SSR was still hanging on.

As far as these soldiers were concerned, the Soviet Union was an idea that remained very much alive. Things might have changed in Moscow. The big bosses in Dushanbe, where Soviet governmental institutions had met into the mid-1990s, might have given up on the socialist dream. But not here. Here at the southern tip of the so-called Special Security Zone, the men of the 201st were assigned to protect the buffer between Tajikistan and Afghanistan. They were holding the line against the Islamist hordes across the river. These Russians would die before they allowed murderous Afghans to infiltrate what they still called (and, more important, thought of as) the USSR.

"Here, in the Soviet Union," one of them told me when I complained about the wait, "we do not jump at the beck and call of journalists."

"But . . . here . . . now . . . isn't . . ." I started. Then I thought better of it.

I hiked my jeans back on and walked back to the car. Floodlights revealed the inky Pyanj River flowing west toward Uzbekistan, where it would debouch into the Amu Darya. During the late 1990s, when Tajikistan was embroiled by civil war, forces loyal to the ex-Communist central government had dumped captured prisoners of the United Tajik

Opposition into the Pyanj, their arms tied together, by the hundreds. (Genocide unfolds in unoriginal ways. The Turks did the same thing to the Armenians.) The drowned Tajiks piled up at a curve of the Amu Darya near Termiz, the site of NATO's post-9/11 airbase in Uzbekistan. Shipping came to a standstill because there were so many corpses clogging the river. The Uzbeks, annoyed at the economic disruption, threatened to invade. But that was two or three years earlier.

On the far side of the river, there was blackness. Afghanistan.

I turned around. Here, in one of the remotest parts of the remotest republic of Central Asia—landlocked, surrounded by huge peaks, off the grid, and diplomatically inaccessible—one could see headlights moving along the Pamir Highway. There was a house. Lights shone out the windows. A couple of streetlights lined the road.

But on the Afghan side: pitch black. It was an international border crossing. Yet: nothing. I'd been to other third world countries, like Thailand and Myanmar. Hell, *Tajikistan* is one of the world's poorest nations. They had electricity. And cars. They had streetlamps and headlights. It was hard for a twenty-first-century person to process the near total blackness of Afghanistan.

I pulled out my Iridium satellite phone. The device was a relic of 1980s design. My hands shivering from the cold, I unfolded its dildo-shaped antenna and waited for a producer at KFI to pick up. KFI was the Los Angeles radio station that had sent me to cover the U.S. invasion. Finally, the call went through. A producer interrupted whatever was airing, played the dramatic "breaking news" lead-in. A swoosh and the collapse of the eight-second broadcast delay announced that I was on the air.

"What's the situation there?" the host asked. It was Bill Handel, the morning drive guy, sounding snide as usual. Was he annoyed at me for breaking into his time? No way to know. He always sounded mean. My producer swore he was a sweetheart. Whatever. It was cold.

Hopping from foot to foot to keep my blood going, trying to generate a little bit of warmth, I explained that *nothing* was going on, that we were stuck at the Tajik-Afghan border waiting for the Russians to unlock the fence so we could board a cable-operated barge across the Pyanj River into Takhar province, which was held half by the Northern Alliance, half by the Taliban. Handel asked me how I got a visa. I explained the weird practice of "Talibanization": both sides in the war honored each other's visas. When I arrived at the front, a Northern Alliance officer would call his Talib counterpart to request a short cease-fire to allow me to cross the battle zone. The Talib would then "Talibanize" my Northern Alliance visa, which I'd been issued in New York, in exchange for thirty dollars, by a bedraggled diplomat who urged me not to go.

Handel asked why my voice sounded quavery. I told him it was because it was *cold*. Which was true.

That's when the bombing began.

Looking back now, I'd guess that the fighting we heard was about a kilometer away. I didn't know that at the time; later experience taught me how to guesstimate. There was a volley of antiaircraft fire (weird, since there wasn't any sign of planes) and lots of small arms. A few dozen shells splashed into the river. I narrated the play-by-play into the phone. Later, when I returned to the United States, KFI listeners wrote to tell me that they couldn't get over the fear in my voice mixed with my attempts to hold it together. Riveting radio! I didn't want to spoil their belief that they had heard something special by admitting that yes, I was scared, but mostly I was just cold. Really, really cold.

Nearly a month later, on the way back out of Afghanistan, I found myself standing in the same spot. Sadoullo was waiting for me. He smiled broadly and waved. If I hadn't been starving and thirsty and wigged out, I would have smiled too. I waved back. Despite everything, I was smiling inside.

I'd made it.

I'd lived through not the worst month of my life but the hardest. Certainly one of the scariest.

You've heard of survivor's guilt. No one talks about survivor's glee, a sense that you got out when others didn't because you were special. At least because you did something right. Unless you want people to think you're a psycho or an asshole or both, it's best not to discuss it unless you're hanging out with a reporter or a combat veteran.

Next to me on the barge across the Pyanj was a wooden box. The box was seven by two by two feet and covered with a forest-green tarp stapled to the top of the sides. It was caked with fine brown dust. The box—the coffin—had been made that morning by a carpenter in the town of Taloqan. He'd wanted forty million afghanis. After the usual haggling, culminating with the customary final explosion of temper that may or may not be pure theater, he settled for thirty.

When it comes down to it, an Afghan carpenter can whip out a coffin pretty quick.

Inside the box lay the body of a Swedish cameraman. His name had been Ulf Strömberg and he was forty-two, married, and the father of three small children. According to the family he'd been staying with, Strömberg had been shot by soldiers, probably Northern Alliance militiamen, fifteen or sixteen years old, in the course of robbing him and three other Swedish journalists of cash and satellite phones. (In press reports in the West, the killers morphed into Talibs.) Strömberg had slammed the door on the robbers, who then fired through the door. He was the third reporter from our convoy to die during our three-week trip.

We owe you an apology. The last several days have revealed severe short-comings in our preparedness to support news organizations in their efforts to cover U.S. military operations in Afghanistan.

—Victoria Clarke, Assistant Secretary of Defense for
Public Affairs, December 2001

Late the day after that freezing night at the border, I was banging around the back of a Soviet-made pickup truck with nine other reporters and perhaps thirty Afghan war entrepreneurs hoping to score work as interpreters, fixers, guides, whatever. Our convoy's original plan had been to pay top dollar—two thousand bucks each—for seats on a Northern Alliance helicopter. It would have been a dazzling half-hour hop across the Hindu Kush to Faizabad, the capital of Badakhshan province, the only district still firmly held by the Northern Alliance by 9/11. Sadly the fog, always a challenge, didn't lift. The chopper didn't fly. Rather than wait around Dushanbe and risk missing the war, we went by land. Clouds of dust, the famous "glacial flour" of Afghanistan, rose up from the vehicles in our convoy as we raced—fifteen miles an hour was racing—across the Chah Ah desert in northern Takhar in a bid to make it to a town before sunset.

Aside from the disgusting sensation of sucking down more dust than had previously entered my lungs during my whole life, my memories of that first day in northern Afghanistan revolve around destruction and mayhem. Adobe ruins stretched to the horizon. Along the horizon, clouds of smoke rose from the ruins of buildings blown up by American bombers. Refugees lugged their possessions on their backs and on carts; as if to underscore the feeling that there was nowhere safe to go, they filed by in both directions.

We passed one bombed-out village after another, each of different vintage. This one had been loyal to the Northern Alliance; the Taliban had bombed it a few years earlier, and now it was a grid of mud walls, grass roofs gone, zillions of shells and shattered antiaircraft guns glimmering amid the ruins. That one had been caught in the crossfire between two warlords—as usual, in the north—and one of them was the notorious Rashid Dostum, the cynical Uzbek warlord who always managed to switch to the winning side at the right moment. This other village had been destroyed by the Russians, rebuilt, then set ablaze, but the Afghans we asked couldn't agree on who was responsible, and anyway, what did it matter, since Allah chooses your time?

It was hot and cold at the same time—and, always, swirling in a world of dust—and where there wasn't a dead village there were Afghan cemeteries, iconic with their piles of stones spiked by sticks, some bearing green and white strips of cloth. (The green flags mark the graves of individuals deemed notable for their wisdom and sagacity, such men being judged in short supply after twenty-three years of civil conflict.) I felt warm wetness on my hands. After hours in Afghanistan, the skin on my knuckles and joints had cracked open. My hands bled, dripping on the floor. Glacial flour caked around the drops.

I rode with three Polish guys from Radio Zet. The Poles kept watchful eyes on their dozen boxes of gear, six of which contained cases of cheap Tajik wine. There was a couple working for Spanish television, based in Moscow, as well as a dude from the U.K. *Independent*. A Russian guy in his forties rounded out our lorry. During the 1980s, the Russian explained, he had served in the Red Army during the occupation of Afghanistan. This was his first time in country since Soviet times, and he claimed he was glad to be back. I expressed surprise. "Look around," he ordered, making a big circle with his arms as we smashed into the zillionth rockhole of the journey. "Of course I am happy. Because this time, *Amerikanski*, all this *shit*"—he broke into a wide gap- and golden-toothed smile and pointed at me—"belongs to *you*."

It was the end of the beginning of the U.S. invasion of Afghanistan. Kunduz, the Taliban government's last bastion in the north, fell a week later. Two weeks after that, Northern Alliance forces entered the militia's southern redoubt of Kandahar. Mullah Omar and his entourage were last seen on motorcycles, heading into the mountains of Uruzgan province. It was over. For the time being.

This is the Afghan way to react to invaders. In 1839, twenty-one thousand British and Indian troops supporting the East India Company occupied Kabul after a few easily won battles. The Afghans melted away into the mountains to hide, study their enemy, and bide their time. Which came in 1842—and the denouement couldn't have been more poetic or disastrous. But the Bush administration officials behind the invasion of Afghanistan didn't study history. They *made* history. That's what they said, anyway, and they seemed to believe it. "We're an empire now," Karl Rove spat infamously, "and when we act, we create our own reality."

Hamid Karzai, a dashing Pashtun who'd gotten to know Bush's Texas crowd as a consultant to the Unocal oil company during the 1990s, was installed as chairman of a provisional government, the new Afghan Interim Authority, on December 22, 2001. This was part of the new reality Bush and his captains created.

Due to the security situation in Afghanistan, the Authority had to meet in Bonn, Germany. America had liberated Afghanistan from the Taliban. But it hadn't conquered them. That was the reality Bush and Rove couldn't change.

The road from the Tajik border to Taloqan was an ordeal for travelers. We banged around the back of our pickup, repeatedly bashing our heads into the sides as we crashed into rocks and holes at crazy angles. Three days later, my headache was still raging and my ears still ringing; I pronounced myself prepared to die before I went back on That Road. Most of us must have suffered concussions.

Not that there was any other way out.

On the first night, en route to Taloqan, we stopped at a house. A fierce-looking old man with a ZZ Top beard and two AKs strapped over his shoulder answered the door.

"Commander's house," my translator—I hadn't hired him yet, but he predicted that I would, and of course he was right—explained. A commander could mean a minor warlord or a major one. "Guest-house."

He showed me a room and separated me from seventy-five dollars. The place was empty and incomplete. Unfinished floors and walls. Poured cement floors. No locks on the door, so I found one of those plastic chairs you see in every café and bar of every country in the developing world and wedged it under the doorknob. People—sounded like Afghans—knocked insistently on the door all night. Scared and stubborn, I ignored the would-be robber-rapist-murderers' pounding and lay in my sleeping bag, too thin for the Afghan winter, grinding my teeth, failing to fend off the cold.

I didn't sleep. It was a long night.

The cost of decades of constant war was evident from the moment I got up in the warlord's unfinished guesthouse and looked out the window—more accurately, the hole in the wall where a window usually goes. Here was the fourteenth century: no power lines, no contrails from jets flying overhead, farmers plowing their soil with emaciated cows, boys tooling about on gaunt donkeys lugging huge bundles of sticks. Conspicuously missing was that barely perceptible but clearly audible layered buzz of life in the industrialized world: devices and machines and invisible waves for radio and wifi and whatnot compiled into a white noise we never notice until we walk down a country road in Vermont or wake up in Afghanistan, where it's the fourteenth century.

Though even in Vermont, you feel the hum.

The fourteenth century looks like mud and smells like cow shit and dust, like a construction site. People work in the fields and walk side by side on dirt paths while talking softly. The sun burns; the air is freezing.

As we prepared to leave, our host grabbed my translator by his *shalwar kameez* and approached me. "He wants to say," he said, "that he tried to bring you a carpet and blankets several times during the night, but you did not open the door. Why?"

Since the bridges had all been blown up, we had to ford the rivers. The always industrious Afghans responded to this demand created by journalists by creating a new line of business; for twenty bucks men on horseback led their steeds back and forth across the rapids in order to find the shallowest point, the best place to cross. The convoy then charged into the water, engines roaring. The water was about four feet deep. Our truck stalled in the middle. In the West, of course, water in your engine is a Major Problem involving Thousands of Dollars. Our driver motioned for us to sit still—where were we going to go? we were in the middle of a river—pulled a few tools from under his seat, and scrambled over his steering wheel (no windshield) to work on the problem. Half an hour later, we were on our way. He had taken the engine apart, blown the water out of the pipes with his lungs, and put the whole thing back together. Wartime Darwinism had killed off the stupid Afghans, if there ever were any.

All along the way, our Afghan drivers improvised to contend with seemingly impassable obstacles. Gaps in the "road" were expertly jury-rigged with branches, disused tank treads, and stones in order to allow vehicles to pass. In the mountains we were asked to lean to one side as the driver floored it over missing sections of "road," two tires hanging miraculously over the abyss, like those *Road Runner* cartoons in which the coyote remains aloft for several seconds before realizing he's out of cliff.

In the last mountain pass before the desert, we encountered a man. Big black beard, fierce eyes, leathery skin, probably an ethnic Tajik.

Here I should clarify ethnicity versus nationality. Everyone who lives in Afghanistan is an Afghan. But there are numerous tribes in Afghanistan, and most people identify themselves as a member of one of the major tribes first and as an Afghan second. Major ethnic groups include Tajiks, Uzbeks, Hazaras, and Pashtuns. (To add to the confusion, a Tajik can also be a Tajikistani, or citizen of Tajikistan. Uzbeks also have a Central Asian republic to call home.) Tajiks speak Dari, derived from tenth-century Persian. About half the country, especially in the southeast, are Pashtuns (as are many Pakistanis). Some Pashtuns dream of creating a "Greater Pashtunistan" that was split by the British-drawn Durand Line, which divides Pakistan and Afghanistan.

The man on the mountain looked about forty-five years old to me, but this was Afghanistan, where people age fast. Probably more like thirty. He squatted above the convoy of foreign reporters, wrapped up in blankets and a turban. At his side was an AK-47. Was this an ambush? Plainly not: he never so much as flinched.

"Look at that guy," marveled the British journalist I'd been shouting back and forth to about geopolitics. "There isn't a human settlement anywhere around here for miles. He got up this morning and thought, 'Hey, I'll go out to the road and see what's going on.' That's his plan for the day. He's not like us, with our deadlines and ambitions. He's got everything he needs. He *is* everything he needs." It occurred to me then, as it often has since, that maybe it was true that that Afghan guy had figured everything out.

Or maybe he wasn't Zen at all. Maybe he'd just had a fight with his wife and needed some fresh air. Still, the Brit's idea of what he was doing, that in-the-moment approach to existence, maybe that's what it's all about.

Three weeks later, my colleague was interviewing a group of Taliban POWs on the side of the road in Kunduz. They set upon him like wolves. They tore the skin off his body with their bare hands. Three days later, he was dead. Infection. The hospital didn't have any supplies—not even Band-Aids, thanks to years of U.S. trade sanctions. (Clinton had denied that medical supplies weren't making it into Afghanistan, but we saw the proof everywhere.)

My new friend had needed skin grafts. We'd tried to get him a spot in a corner of a Northern Alliance chopper heading back to Tajikistan, where my fixer had arranged for a military hospital to treat him, but local Afghan commanders and senior warlords informed reporters that then Defense Secretary Donald Rumsfeld had forbidden America's new Afghan allies from assisting journalists in any way. Medevacs were specifically proscribed. That didn't leave many good options. In his state the Brit would never have survived the trip back up That Road. We buried him in the soccer field adjacent to the Red Crescent hospital.

There's a town called Khwaja Ghar about halfway to Taloqan. We arrived there around three in the afternoon. After hours of dust and desert and searing, dry heat, we were pleasantly surprised to find buildings that hadn't been destroyed. As we drew nearer, we noticed a square mud-and-log watchtower improvised over an abandoned local school, surrounded by razor wire and sandbags. A couple of soldiers gazed down at us impassively. Above them from a tree limb flapped the white flag of the Taliban government.

Across the street a boy about eight or nine years of age stood on the roof of his house. He waved. We waved back. He smiled a sweet smile. He picked up an AK-47, aimed it at us, and squeezed off a few rounds. We were so dazed from the ride that we didn't flinch. It was surreal: a peaceful scene in which a cute-as-the-dickens kid was trying to murder us. And we didn't react. Two older men ambled over, tugged the gun out of his hands, and walked away. The boy howled and cried. What was wrong with me? I felt almost sorry for the little thug with bad aim.

Our driver hesitated. Retreat or press on? He floored it. We entered town.

High walls topped with shards of glass lined the streets. When you can't call the cops because there are no cops, turning your house into a fortress is Plan B. Doors were tiny and armored with metal plates. No doorknobs on the outside. Medieval security at its best; every man's home was his little castle, a set of walls surrounding compounds of small buildings. The roads were muck and dust. A couple of sad-looking stores selling such staples as Pakistani soft drinks and matches. No cars. Lots of donkeys and mud—did I mention the mud?—and donkey shit. A row of tank treads served as impromptu speed bumps—not that many cars could handle those streets at high speed.

As the sun arced toward the horizon, and the cosmopolitan pleasures of Khwaja Ghar faded in our nonexistent rearview mirrors, our driver sped up. The whole convoy followed suit. Our bone-jarring ride again became a backbreaking one. After a few minutes of this I scrambled over the Tajik wine boxes and yelled at the driver. "Slow down! It's terrible back here!" I shouted. He hit the gas.

His comrade in the front seat—a ferret-faced young man who I later learned was a sixteen-year-old ex-Talib trying to go underground in the wake of recent political changes—turned and shouted at me in English, "We must be in Taloqan before dark. If not, we will all be killed." This was the sort of thing Afghans liked to say: blah blah blah or you will get killed. Fatalism can be fun.

"Why?" I asked. "The people hate reporters that much?"

"It has nothing to do with you being reporters," he explained. "Everyone who is outside after dark is killed. If he is lucky, he is not raped first."

This was later confirmed by people of all ages and ethnic groups all over Afghanistan. I met middle-aged people who had never been outside the walls of their compounds after dusk. In the coming days I would huddle inside my rented walls and listen to terrible screams coming from outside. Screams and gunshots and laughter and—the worst—silence and vanishing chuckles in Dari.

At night, vampires come.

We arrived in the city of Taloqan in early evening, exhausted, our brains splitting from migraines, caked with dust, as the sun was setting. The Taliban logo on the side of the local school was half painted over. "They started to remove it when the Americans said they were coming," said the English-speaking ex-/maybe-not-ex-Talib. "But then someone heard on the radio that they only sent eight hundred American soldiers for the whole country. So the Taliban might come back."

Seemed like a smart assessment of the situation. The 2001 U.S. invasion of Afghanistan was primarily an air campaign. The Air Force dropped millions of pounds of ordnance on positions they believed to be held by the Taliban. But, aside from the first vapor trails of the trip, from B-52s circling tens of thousands of feet above, where the white "sky people" (as Afghans called them, and we reporters bought into) decided who would live or die without seeing them, actual American soldiers were nowhere to be seen. About eight hundred U.S. Special Forces troops were up in the mountains, hanging out with Northern Alliance militia leaders they'd bribed with bricks of new hundred-dollar bills wrapped in cellophane, calling in air strikes based on the directions of men who couldn't read and whose motivations were opaque. There were a lot of mistakes—a lot of dead civilians and dead allies—but the air war worked. With the exceptions of the battles of Kunduz—which we were there to witness—and Kandahar in the south, Taliban lines crumbled when the first U.S. missiles struck. What the Americans didn't seem to know, and the Afghans didn't tell them, was that this is the Afghan way: when heavily armed invaders arrive, they fade away. Years pass, prompting the invader turned occupier to believe that he holds a firm grip on a passive populace. Then the Afghans begin picking them off. They're relentless. Eventually, after more time passes, the occupiers calculate that Afghanistan isn't worth it. They trim back their occupation budget. Finally they leave. It was the same in 1713, 1842, 1880, 1919, and 1989.

Kabul fell less than two months after the beginning of the U.S. invasion. There wasn't much of a battle. The United States fired cruise missiles and dropped two-thousand-pound bombs onto the capital until the Taliban withdrew.

Which is not to say they left.

> Who are the combatants in guerrilla warfare? On one side we have a group composed of the oppressor and his agents, the professional army, well armed and disciplined, in many cases receiving foreign help as well as the help of the bureaucracy in the employ of the oppressor. On the other side are the people of the nation or region involved. It is important to emphasize that guerrilla warfare is a war of the masses, a war of the people. The guerrilla band is an armed nucleus, the fighting vanguard of the people. It draws its great force from the mass of the people themselves. The guerrilla band is not to be considered inferior to the army against which it fights simply because it is inferior in firepower. Guerrilla warfare is used by the side which is supported by a majority but which possesses a much smaller number of arms for use in defense against oppression. The guerrilla fighter needs full help from the people of the area. This is an indispensable condition.
>
> —Che Guevara, *General Principles of Guerrilla Warfare*

Rather than broad-stroke, openly declared state-against-state wars, America now fights little "savage wars of peace," as the neoconservative pundit Max Boot called them. At this writing the United States is engaged in active military operations in Somalia, Libya, Mali, Niger, Sudan, Yemen, Pakistan, the Philippines, and Haiti. The principal dynamic of these conflicts is radically different from the World War II scenario. On the Pacific and Western fronts, most of the fighting by American troops occurred in occupied territory, not on the home territory of the principal combatants. This naturally led to relatively well defined front lines and combat zones.

The United States is still huge. To paraphrase Norma Desmond in *Sunset Boulevard*, since World War II, it's war that has gotten small. Since 1945 the United States has invaded only smaller, poorer, virtually defenseless nations. Unsurprisingly, the superpower trounces the enemy. As we saw in Iraq in 2003, the existing nation-state usually collapses within days. The defeated country's armed forces—"shocked and awed" by overwhelming technological and numerical superiority, not to mention utter ruthlessness—scatters. The United States prematurely declares victory and turns its attention to other matters, such as its next war.

It's after the Americans settle in, during the occupation stage, that the war begins in earnest. On one side, we have the United States and its locally appointed puppet government. They are soon challenged by an indigenous resistance, typically a loose alliance of soldiers loyal to the defeated regime and various guerrilla factions organized in response to the occupation. (After the eventual U.S. withdrawal, civil conflict typically breaks out between factions of the local resistance.)

Stripped to the essentials, it comes down to foreigners versus locals. Or foreigners plus local lackeys versus locals.

In these contests the occupier enjoys lopsided advantages of wealth and weapons technology. Yet, perversely, those are rarely enough to win in the long run. Local resistance forces live in the war zone. Locals don't have to, and can't, retreat behind fortresses surrounded by blast walls; they plant their improvised explosive devices, go out for tea, and go home. They don't have to wonder whom they can trust; they know the language, the terrain, and the people better than the best-educated foreign scholar. They know which tactics will instill fear and which will spark contempt. The occupier, on the other hand, is on a tight schedule. As he burns through billions of dollars in cash and matériel, editors and producers in the media and eventually ordinary voters become impatient. They demand results. They want victory. Or at least "peace with honor" (dignified withdrawal). But military and civilian leaders are in too deep, seeing withdrawal as an insult to the lives and treasure invested so far and thus unable, like a gambler, to cut their losses and walk away. What would victory look like? Why are we still there? They don't know.

Indigenous resistance fighters lose almost every engagement. So why are they winning? Because they have all the time in the world. They also have an ace in the hole: the harder the United States hits them, the more of them they kill, the more civilians die. This radicalizes moderates and fence sitters who previously tried to avoid taking sides. Such is the paradox of the occupier: nonviolence isn't politically viable, and brutality is counterproductive.

Because guerrillas choose the time and place and methods of waging a war of resistance against a foreign invader, the occupier—though rich and impossible to defeat via technological means, and heavily engaged in the looting of whatever natural resources it can get its hands on—is invariably disadvantaged. Resistance forces act; occupiers react.

History shows that it is possible to invade, occupy, and ultimately annex foreign territory. Well, it used to be possible. Until and through the nineteenth century, it happened all the time. Every square inch of the United States was seized by direct or indirect force or military coercion, culminating in the 1893 invasion by U.S. marines of the Kingdom of Hawaii. But history also teaches us another lesson: the long-term outcome is often something less than victory. Since the beginning of the twentieth century, however, no nation-state has successfully invaded another—i.e., settled into an unopposed occupation or one that did not continue until the invading nation was forced to withdraw.

The United States exerts influence. It doesn't annex territory. Let's not make Afghanistan/Somalia/whatever's problems ours, goes the thinking. We'll go in with a "light footprint," in military parlance. Yet the occupation without annexation model doesn't work . . . at least not in the long run.

U.S. forces and their Afghan allies in the Northern Alliance met little Taliban resistance during the fall of 2001. Why should the Taliban have fought back? The Americans enjoyed overwhelming military superiority. To resist would have meant suicide. So the Talibs melted away. Some went home and prepared to transition to civilian lives, biding their time until a viable resistance could be organized. Others fled to outposts high in the mountains, where Predator drones can't peer into every cave and crevice, and others fled over the mountains to Waziristan and Pakistan's "Northern Areas" (Pakistani-controlled Kashmir province).

Though driven out of power and fearful of America's proto-shock-and-awe bombing campaign, the Taliban took solace in the realization that they were the future of Afghanistan. Like other local resistance forces driven underground by better-equipped foreign occupiers, the Taliban rallied when they saw that the United States was going to make a lot of mistakes. The Americans' pet Afghan government was a regime headed by a man with little political power or tribal support; moreover, it was woefully underfunded. The U.S. military made little effort to restore law and order in the cities, villages, and remote roads between them. Reconstruction was all talk, no bulldozer.

Sooner rather than later, the Taliban hoped and expected, the United States would come off as culturally insensitive. Brutal. Clueless. Their Afghan allies, recruited from the riffraff of the exile community, would appear meek, bought off, and corrupt. The vast majority of Afghans, ordinary people trying to get by from day to day in one of the world's poorest nations, would pass through the stages of hope, disappointment, disgust, alienation, and finally the rage that prompts a man to take up arms—an easy choice in a country where war has been the biggest economic sector for decades.

Then there was the trump card: occupation is humiliating. The Taliban weren't popular everywhere—far from it—but they were Afghans. Neither the Americans nor the Karzai regime (because it was bought and paid for) could say that.

The Taliban didn't have to print leaflets. The occupation itself would be their recruitment pitch. By 2009, Mullah Mohammed Omar, the Taliban leader exiled in Quetta, Pakistan, was taunting the United States: "You and your allies are facing an absolute defeat, and nothing will change that even if you send more troops, no matter what your strategies are, because the logic of force will have no impact on the mujahideen [formerly the term for anti-Soviet jihadis during the 1980s, now the umbrella term for anti-American fighters] and you will never be able to control the Afghan people by physical force or by your satanic hypocrisy." Such a way with words.

In late November 2001, however, the United States' attempt to subjugate Afghanistan through force of arms was just beginning. The outcome was predictable, yet hardly clear. The Taliban was about to lose its status as a government. It remained in control of two redoubts, Kunduz in the north and Kandahar in the south.

I would spend most of the next three weeks covering the battle of Kunduz. It was a remarkable episode in military history, including an old-fashioned cavalry charge by Alliance horsemen against Taliban tanks, the capture of "American Talib" Johnny Walker Lindh, and a classic tragedy of treachery and miscommunication.

Kunduz, capital of the province of the same name, is just east of

Mazar-i-Sharif, Afghanistan's second-largest city and the key to the control of the northern half of the country in part because it's situated just south of the Termiz border crossing with Uzbekistan, where the bridge by which the USSR invaded is. Mazar was more or less firmly under Northern Alliance control in November 2001. But Kunduz blocked the way to the strangely shaped Wakhan Corridor, the thin strip of land that sticks out toward China. Wakhan, also known as Badakhshan, had remained Northern Alliance throughout the civil war. The north couldn't be unified without Kunduz.

Rashid Dostum, the Uzbek warlord, painstakingly negotiated the surrender of the approximately twenty thousand Taliban government soldiers and several thousand foreign (mostly Pakistani) fighters in Kunduz. This was accomplished in the usual Afghan way. When the probable outcome of a battle is clear, the two sides try to settle the defeat without fighting.

Along with other reporters, we cooled our heels on the outskirts of the city, awaiting the results of the negotiations.

A sitdown was negotiated via satellite phone. "Over cups of tea and biscuits, the terms of the surrender were agreed: all the Afghan fighters trapped in Kunduz would be allowed to go home," reported a writer for the U.K. *Guardian* who managed to listen in. "The Arabs, however, would be taken to General Dostum's mansion, where they would be sorted out into terrorists and non-terrorists, and then their fate would be decided."

That night the skies filled with the roar of planes. As we would later learn, the CIA wanted to save their top-level assets—i.e., the biggest terrorists. Two Pakistani Air Force Hercules C-130s, operating under U.S. supervision, ferried the Pakistanis, including members of Al Qaeda, over the mountains to Pakistan. The evacuation accomplished, the two sides agreed to declare Kunduz an open city. But not all the Taliban commanders got word of the deal. When jubilant

Northern Alliance forces moved into the city, the Talibs opened fire. Dostum's men interpreted this act as a betrayal. Swearing revenge, they organized the systemic massacre of up to eight thousand Taliban POWs over the course of a weekend in a desolate patch of desert called Dasht-i-Leili. "These men were murdered in a grotesque fashion, summarily executed and kicked into large holes in the ground with American soldiers standing by," Jamie Doran, a journalist and director who investigated the massacre, told me.

A twelve-man U.S. Fifth Special Forces Group unit, Operational Detachment Alpha 595, guarded the prison's front gates. "Everything was under the control of the American commanders," a Northern Alliance soldier told Doran. American troops searched the bodies for Al Qaeda identification cards. "Some of [the prisoners] were [still] alive," a Pakistani driver pressed into service to ship the prisoners recalled. "They were shot" while "maybe thirty or forty" American soldiers watched.

By the time I arrived at the site, the detritus of the murders—shell casings, human bones, and clothes of the victims—went on farther than I could see.

(In 2009, newly elected president Obama pledged to order an investigation. He never did.)

I returned from Afghanistan with what I think must have been post-traumatic stress syndrome—I was never formally diagnosed, but I guess that's what it was. At the time that I crossed the border into Afghanistan, however, I was thrilled to be there, albeit disappointed that it had taken so long to get inside. It was my fourth trip to post-Soviet Central Asia, a region that had enthralled me since my first journey to research a travel-adventure piece for a men's magazine about driving the Silk Road from Beijing to Istanbul. The Turkic-speaking dictatorships of Turkmenistan, Uzbekistan, and Kazakhstan were at once maddening and bemusingly bizarre to travel through. Kyrgyzstan, with its poor but friendly people, and the only democratically elected president in the region, featured stunning mountains and rushing streams. Tajikistan, the poorest state in the former Soviet Union, was a cultural cul-de-sac, an odd-man-out whose language derived from tenth-century Persian. But it was Afghanistan that remained the most daunting: dangerous, polyglot, and still so remote that reliable maps were hard to come by.

When the war broke out following the September 11 attacks, I sat at home watching the skimpy coverage on CNN and other cable news channels. I knew from my previous journeys that much of what was being transmitted to the American public was either incomplete or wrong. The Taliban, according to media accounts, identified themselves with black long-tailed turbans. (It's a tribal identifier, and many men unaffiliated with the Taliban were mistakenly targeted for air strikes because of this mistake.) The training camps were for anti-American terrorists. (They were actually for jihadis of all stripes. Most of them fought in other countries, such as China and Russia.)

I was itching to get over there and find out the truth—I told everyone I wanted to get the truth for the public, which was true, but what I really cared about was getting the real story for myself. So I went to my program director at KFI, the radio station in Los Angeles for whom I was doing a political talk show, to suggest that they send me to cover it. They agreed, but budgeted only half of the twenty grand I thought I'd need. For a desperately poor country with one hundred percent unemployment, I liked to say, it sure was an expensive travel destination. Because journalists were always being gouged for everything from housing to transportation to security, wads of one-hundred-dollar bills were required every day. For the other ten thousand I pitched my editor at *The Village Voice*, for whom I drew cartoons and wrote features.

I wasn't the only would-be war correspondent looking for trouble in the Hindu Kush. First the *Voice* sent a guy who spent weeks running up a bar tab at the Islamabad Marriott before he realized that the Khyber Pass wasn't going to open before the war was over. Then—this is my favorite story—they sent a dude who got himself proto-embedded (there was no formal embedding program yet) with the U.S. Navy—this for covering the invasion of a landlocked country. The guy spent a month on that ship, and in his defense he did manage to send in some cool shots of cruise missiles getting fired off an aircraft carrier in the Indian Ocean. But that was as close as he got. Missed the whole war. Or so he—and his editor—thought.

Finally I was anointed the *Voice*'s C-list Afghanistan correspondent. My pitch was simple: "I can get in." I didn't mention how: through Tajikistan, where the border never closed, because it was used by Northern Alliance warlords to truck in U.N.-banned armaments supplied by their Russian patrons and to export illicit Afghan rubies. So the *Voice* said yes. But not because they respected me. I was C-list for a reason.

They didn't know anyone else crazy or stupid enough to try for the crap money they were willing to pay.

True, flying into Tajikistan was in fact a pain in the ass—which is why the idea didn't occur to many U.S. media outlets. At the time, Tajikistan had consular representation in only three other countries, none of them in the Western hemisphere. To get into this former Soviet republic you paid four hundred bucks at the Russian embassy for a document you could purportedly present at the airport to be admitted into the capital; then you had twenty-four hours to get a real Tajik visa from the Ministry of Foreign Affairs or face arrest by the KGB, as long as it wasn't a holiday or they simply didn't feel like opening for business that day. Once you arrived, assuming you hadn't been deported for lack of a proper visa, you needed permission from the Ministry to enter a one-hundred-kilometer-wide "exclusion zone" along the Tajik-Afghan border. But rejection was certain unless your bribe got into the right pair of hands. Oh, and there was only one flight a week. You flew into Moscow's Sheremetyevo-2 international airport, then took a hundred-buck taxi ride to the crappy little new airport at Domodedovo, all the way on the other side of the Russian capital's vast urban sprawl, to catch a Tajik Air flight—pressurization optional, loose wires hanging from the ceiling, smoking flight attendants, drunken pilots, meals a must to avoid—to the Tajik capital, Dushanbe.

Upon arrival in Dushanbe, reporters were shunted into the sad Hotel Tajikistan, a hideous Soviet-era hulk with cold-water showers running rusty mud-sludge so thick that you could sculpt your hair with it after bathing. Next you could try to catch the chopper to the Northern Alliance's high-altitude redoubt in Badakhshan. Winding through snowy mountain passes was, by most accounts, an unforgettable experience. "If you see the vapor trail [of a Stinger missile] coming toward you," a colleague advised, "suck in the view because it's the last thing you'll ever see." Such downings were not uncommon.

Heavy fog kept the chopper grounded for days, so rather than spend the war consuming Tajik mystery meat and vodka from plastic bottles in Dushanbe, I decided to join a convoy of cars and trucks for a land crossing. My fixer got me a cute sedan with a cracked windshield and off we went, banging down dirt tracks toward the Tajik-Afghan border.

I lost track of how many times my head smacked into the roof.

As we stepped off the barge on the Afghan side of the Pyanj, scruffy fighters draped with bandoliers herded us into a small house furnished with boxes of ammunition, a kerosene lamp, and a freshly installed customs officer whose illiteracy was evidenced by his stamping our passports upside down. Once we were outside, enterprising drivers proposed to drive us to the next town. For twelve hundred dollars.

Network TV crews each peeled off a dozen hundreds and roared off into the night inside brand-new SUVs freshly stolen from god knows where—though they had factory stickers from Dubai. Having been to Afghanistan before—and on a limited budget—I tried to argue the dwindling number (and quality) of drivers down to something approaching what I thought was fair: a buck or two.

"How far is it?" I asked.

"Maybe twenty kilometers," one driver answered.

About twelve miles. "I'll wait until morning," I said. "I can walk."

They were appalled. "You can't walk!" my driver said.

"Why not? I just came around the entire world! Twenty kilometers is nothing."

I watched the gears turn in their heads. It dawned on me that these guys didn't have any idea how big the world was, much less how far we had traveled to get there.

Hours passed. Finally, the last driver and I struck a deal for forty dollars. I was still pretty angry about it. Two months' pay for a twenty-minute ride in a fourth-world shithole was beyond ridiculous.

At this point I should mention that the guys from ABC and the other big TV networks arrived at the warlord's guesthouse about an hour after me. "It sure is a long ride," a producer told me.

"What are you talking about? Maybe twenty minutes," I said.

"We've been driving through the mountains for the last four hours," he replied. "Pure hell."

I would've laughed if I'd had the energy. To justify their twelve-hundred-dollar taxi rides, the Afghans had taken them around in circles half the night.

Upon arrival in Taloqan, our convoy of reporters was surrounded by Afghans offering accommodations. A hundred bucks a day scored me a freezing-cold room in a private house containing a stained carpet infested with bed lice and a couple of grotty tatami mats along the walls. The compound, which belonged to a pharmacist, was across a muddy street from the local Red Crescent hospital. My host charged five bucks for the wood to heat up a bucket of water for a *hamam* (bath), plus a dollar an egg. Otherwise, food was included. Since it was Ramadan, however, no food was sold during the day. At night, you'd have to go out—but who'd take the risk? Wars should be scheduled with more consideration for those who report them.

The décor of my lodgings reflected the rapidly shifting politics of the time: two posters issued by the United Arab Emirates tourism board extolling the architectural landmarks of Dubai. According to the pharmicist's young son, the Talib junior official who had let the room before me had put them up before fleeing. Prostitute- and booze-filled Dubai was a playground for Islamists looking to cut loose after a hard week flogging slutty women at the Ministry for the Promotion of Virtue and the Prevention of Vice. My window looked out into a small dusty (what else?) courtyard. In the middle was a small garden. There were two rocks, painted red, in the garden. A mine was underneath, one of an estimated five to ten million scattered around the country after decades of war. A reporter told me that they looked like OZM-72s, from Russia. The design of the OZM-72 was modeled on the "Bouncing Betty," a German mine feared by GIs because it bounces several feet up in the air before exploding. The target is the genitals.

Who puts a mine in the courtyard of a house?

Across the hall from my room was one let by Lois Romano of *The Washington Post*. She was the first Western reporter to get into Taloqan, riding in on top of a Northern Alliance armored personnel carrier. Lois looked to be in her mid-forties. She was tough, funny, and sweet at the same time, the perfect combination in a war zone—the kind of person you feel comfortable around instantly. You'd never know she'd only been there a week. Her room was outfitted with carpets and tribal war hangings from the local bazaar. There was something that separated us, though: the class distinction between her huge corporate paper and my smaller corporate one. Unlike the *Voice*, her employer took interest in her well-being. Every now and then a young Afghan man would arrive asking for Lois. He bore gifts: bricks of shrinkwrapped hundred-dollar bills, courtesy of the *Post*. There were no mod cons anywhere in town except the local warlord's compound (so I heard from the ABC News crew that stayed there), no running water or real toilets or heat and of course no electricity, but Lois had a high-end generator the size of a rider mower going twenty-four seven. Sometimes she let me charge my devices in her room, which saved me a long wait at the hospital.

I settled in quickly as well. At 4:30 or 5:00 I would awake to the cry of my host family's rooster, a cruel animal that curled into a ball in front of a muddy hole serving as an outhouse. It awoke instantly in a blur of screams and ferocious pecks whenever you tried to step over it. I tried to avoid these nocturnal adventures; sadly, nature calls often when you're suffering from Afghan diarrhea. If by happenstance the rooster forgot to crow, festive Pakistani film soundtrack music played by family members enjoying their last meal of the day before the Ramadan fast fixed that. I'd stumble out into the street to place a satellite call to KFI's afternoon drive show, *John and Ken*, in order to report on the military situation—which I knew next to nothing about, since there was no TV or radio there—and my impressions of the general state of affairs.

Since we were the only two people awake and out on the street so early, I soon made friends with the proprietor of the local convenience store, a tiny shack whose total stock couldn't have fetched a hundred bucks. He was an old man with an impressive gray beard and a huge mole on his left cheek. Protruding from the mole was a two-foot-long hair. (This, in case you didn't know, is a Thing in some Asian countries. In China and Thailand and I assume elsewhere, long hairs sticking out of a mole used to be considered a sign of wisdom. Apparently they still are. I don't know if Westerners have whatever it takes to grow them.) He was probably in his fifties, and he had benefited from the Communist regime's requirement that students learn English. Every morning he asked me who I was, where I was from, and what I was doing, and we went from there. After about a week of getting acquainted, he asked me: "Why do you look at this?" He pointed at his mole.

"I can't help wondering," I said, "how it survived so many years of war when so many other things are gone." He seemed to like that.

One morning the old man motioned me to come closer. He moved the box he was sitting on and yanked open a trapdoor in the floor of his shack. He yanked out a case of Pepsi. "Here," he said, "just pay me the usual rate [of about a dime a can]." It was a rare find, a precious gift. Because food was available only at night, when we couldn't go out, we hadn't eaten anything substantial since our arrival. We'd managed to scrounge an undated pack of bottles of carbonated orange soda called Ashi-Mashi, supposedly made in Pakistan. But it was hard to take, so sickeningly sweet and fake orangey that we couldn't keep it down.

I read the label on one of the cans of Pepsi. Qatari. 1995. The shopkeeper had kept this stash hidden under the floor of his little shop through six years of civil conflict, only to give it to me. I savored the moment. *Drink*, he motioned. I pulled off the old-fashioned pull tab. Pssh! Still carbonated. There was a little rust around the rim. I took a sip. America. It tasted like *America*. And it had caffeine. My mood— and the quality of my writing—instantly improved.

I commuted to the front alongside my fixer, Jovid. It was just shy of forty miles from Taloqan to the eastern Kunduz front in the hamlet of Khanabad. The road hadn't been maintained since the Soviet period, but it was great by local standards. It existed. You could make it hundreds of feet without having to stop to deal with, say, a river. Or a bomb crater. The one-way trip only took about two hours.

You could see the Taliban line about a kilometer farther west, down the road toward Kunduz. We were bored most of the time. Reporters from Russia and Spain and Argentina and Germany milled about, snapping photographs of the vapor trails of the B-52s circling overhead. Every now and then there would be an explosion along the base of the mountains, where there were villages, to the south of the highway. *Poof.* Like a brick thudding into the sand. A cloud of dust would rise. The photographers clicked away.

Our translators warned that the Northern Alliance soldiers were plotting to rob us. I would have robbed me too. I carried thousands of dollars in cash. And I was one of the poor reporters! "The stingy American," the Afghans called me because I insisted on negotiating for everything. The TV guys paid whatever was demanded. They each had at least a hundred grand, which they flashed around too much. They attracted a lot of attention.

The soldiers were dirt poor, kids mostly, and they carried AK-47s and RPGs. I figured *inshallah*, if they want to rob us, they will, and there's nothing we can do about it, so why worry?

I'd lived in New York all my adult life. I've got reliable instincts; anyone who lived there through the 1980s does. I can feel the distinct buzz of a group of people getting itchy to attack you. Whenever the vibration got louder, we got some help from Taliban snipers. *Poof, poof, poof.* Puffs of glacial flour rose from the ground where AK bullets struck. At first we flinched. Most reporters soon realized that there was no point. By the time you hear a gunshot, it has already hit or missed.

Everything is *inshallah*. You could hide behind a wall, but then you wouldn't see anything coming.

More worrisome were mortars and bombs. The mortars came courtesy of the Taliban; as mortars do, they fell closer each time. Every other day we'd move our staging area to prevent them from calibrating their target. Our security measures weren't quite enough. One afternoon, minutes after I'd left for Taloqan, a mortar fell near one of my colleagues. No one knew where the guy was from, just that he was a TV person. It wasn't a direct hit, but it didn't matter; the spray of rocks went through him like a hail of bullets. Since he was working independently, as a freelancer, no one claimed his corpse. A Northern Alliance commander ordered his men to bury him between a minefield and the journalists' parking area.

Night fell around five, so I left around three. We wove between refugees and donkey carts and tanks and APCs, our driver leaning on the horn the whole time, South Asian movie soundtrack drivel blaring from one working speaker. I took advantage of the chance to charge my sat phone with the car's cigarette lighter while placing calls to the States. Hanging out the window because the sat signal wouldn't work otherwise (gotta point to the sky!), chaos all around, I felt like Marky Mark in the Gulf War movie *Three Kings*. I called my mom to wish her a happy Thanksgiving. She was a high school French teacher; there'd been some workplace drama. When she was done telling her story about a bitchy colleague, I informed her that I had to go. "It's seven dollars a minute," I told her. That one call cost me three hundred twenty bucks. "You never care about my stories," she replied, not believing me. "You only want to talk about yourself!"

Back in Taloqan, my evening routine revolved around three activities: writing, reporting, and trying to get warm. This last item revolved around the only source of available heat: a benzene-fueled hurricane lamp. As the temperature plunged from ninety to sixty to thirty within an hour after sunset, we huddled around and rubbed our hands over it. It was a devil's choice: choke on toxic fumes or freeze to death. We alternated. Heat. Breathe. Heat. Breathe.

I wrote a couple of hours a day. Since there was no reliable source of electricity with which to power a laptop, I used a battery-operated Palm electronic organizer in conjunction with a foldout keyboard to report the day's events. Then I'd step into the street to call the *Voice*.

I imagine it has since been eliminated, along with cartoons, international and national politics, and news—not to mention political commentary—but in 2001 *The Village Voice* still maintained the old-fashioned position of dictation clerk.

Reading three thousand words of tiny text from the Palm over the phone to the woman assigned to transcribe was a pain in the ass. The clock was clicking: not only was the phone call killing my budget, the battery on the sat phone lasted only forty-five minutes at best. At three thousand words, a dictation could easily use up that time. Curious locals gathered around, asking questions, threatening, wanting to call their displaced relatives all over the world. Not to mention the fact that I was standing out in the middle of the street. At night. At a bare minimum I worried that someone would steal my phone. The woman in New York managed to make a bad situation worse.

"Can you spell that?" she asked me about the word "Taliban."

"T-A-L-I-B-A-N. New paragraph: Clashes in Kunduz province—"

"Can you spell that?"

"Please, no, can you look it up? Later, after you hang up? My battery is about to run out. Have Dan copyedit it. I have to—"

"What's that?"

"What's what?"

"Those sounds! I can't hear you. Tell whoever it is to keep it down."

"That's a battle. Gunfire. There's a helicopter landing field a hundred meters down the street."

More editing. More interruptions. The transcriber made me hold while she chatted up a colleague. "How was your date? Was he cute?"

I can still hear her saying it: *key-yewwwt.*

I was losing it. "Do you mind? I'm in a fucking *war*! Gossip on your own fucking time!"

She let out a big sarcastic Long Island sigh. "Can I ask you something?"

"Who could stop you?"

"What?"

"Never mind. What is it?"

"I don't understand something."

"What's that?"

"Why don't you just fax in your story? You know, from Kinko's?"

How could I explain the fourteenth century to someone whose world was New York, the suburbs surrounding New York, the transportation arteries between New York and its suburbs? I watched and observed and drew conclusions, which I discussed over the radio and published in the *Voice* and compiled into a book titled *To Afghanistan and Back.* But no one understood. No one ever would.

How could I explain, for example, the insanity of carpet bombing? Or even that it was happening?

Every night, old-fashioned B-52s, the same old planes that bombed Vietnam to smithereens, dropped thousands of bombs all over Afghanistan. They fell willy-nilly, as bombs do, and killed lots of people that we'll never know about, and as far as the media were concerned, it was as though it had never happened. They were there. They saw it. Somehow the carpet bombing didn't fit in with the post-Kosovo narrative that America was now fighting precision wars using smart bombs that only blew up the very worst people in the ugliest, least architecturally significant buildings.

Back home in the States, the war was incessantly portrayed as a gentle, low-key, high-precision aerial campaign in which the United States targeted evil Talibs in telltale black long-tail turbans using sophisticated technology that could read the date on a penny from six miles up in order to spare the lives of the innocent Afghans we were there to liberate. Americans watched cameras mounted on million-dollar missiles shoot down the chimneys of supposed Taliban safehouses and went to sleep at night, confident that their taxes weren't being misspent on random pell-mell genocide (you know, like Vietnam).

Six weeks into the war, the *Los Angeles Times* was one of countless media outlets still measuring Afghanistan's national civilian casualty count in double digits: "Although estimates are still largely guesses, some experts believe that more than 1,000 Taliban and opposition troops have probably died in the fighting, along with at least dozens of civilians."

Dozens.

Twelve and a half time zones forward and a day before that piece appeared, the Air Force dropped a BLU-82 "daisy cutter" bomb on a bridge about fifty feet long south of Khanabad. This event took place in the middle of the night. The blast set off a seismic event that shook us up two dozen miles to the east where we were sleeping. The ground rumbled for about a minute. Windows shattered. Dogs went nuts. A blast of heat passed through mudbrick walls. First we thought it was an earthquake. Then we wondered if we'd felt the blast of a nuclear weapon.

Dozens of daisy cutters wreaked havoc on Afghanistan during the fall of 2001. This single incident left at least five hundred fifty people dead. That was the total number of torsos pulled out of the rubble. There was no way to determine whether, say, a stray hand represented a discrete or duplicate casualty count. This carnage was a daily occurrence for many months. Tens, possibly hundreds, of thousands of Afghans perished during the initial phase of the U.S. invasion from fall 2001 to spring 2002. The Air Force dropped at least twenty-two thousand bombs weighing a total of eight thousand six hundred tons. Exact figures for cruise missiles are unknown, but they were used frequently. The United States also unleashed thousands of "cluster bombs," a device that releases canister mines painted brightly in order to attract the attention of children. Each CBU-87 "mother bomb" releases two hundred two bomblets from a few hundred feet above the ground; these are carried by small parachutes. Each bomblet is designed to fragment into three hundred steel shards. Each CBU-87 thus carries more than sixty thousand individual projectiles.

Back in the United States, audiences were thrilling to "smart bombs" with laser-guided targeting. That's not what we were seeing. Every evening between six and nine p.m. American planes rained three-hundred-dollar "dumb bombs" on the western outskirts of Taloqan. On the fifth or sixth night of this campaign I accompanied a cameraman for ABC to witness the carnage. What we saw, and he videotaped, was unspeakable: deafening explosions, great clouds of dust and smoke, flames higher than the buildings they replaced, bits and pieces of cloth and flesh in odd places, e.g., half a rib cage hanging from a tree branch. The cameraman filled up one Betamax tape after another and tossed them into his duffel bag. On the walk back to the center of town I asked the ABC guy if he needed time to set up a satellite uplink in order to send the footage to New York. He replied no, that these were for his personal use, not the network's, that imagery like this would and could never appear on television in the United States. "If the American people saw what bombing looked like on the ground," he explained, "they would riot in the streets. It would be banned." Which would be the end of American foreign policy.

The nightly bombings continued. We found this surprising. After all, it had been widely reported that Taloqan was under Northern Alliance control. Not completely—the Taliban still ran the firehouse and its 1920s-vintage horse-drawn fire engine—but as far as these things went, you couldn't ask for a place that less needed to be carpet bombed. Finally (I think it was almost two weeks in), we decided to phone the Pentagon.

A late arrival from *The New York Times* made the call. He called +1-202-555-1212, Washington information, and asked for a main number for the Department of Defense.

"Hello," the *Times* man said. "I'm in Taloqan, in Takhar province, in northern Afghanistan near the Kunduz front. You are bombing our position, but we are in territory controlled by the Northern Alliance, who are an American ally. I need to talk to someone in charge of the war." He listened. "Uh-huh," he said. "I see. Are you sure? Okay, then."

He looked at us. "It was a night receptionist. They've gone home for the night. They promised to leave a note for the appropriate people."

Okay, I wouldn't have put him through either. Desperate reporters do foolish things.

The bombing continued. Right on time, six to nine, every night. Maybe no one read the right yellow stickie.

Upon my return I described Afghanistan's shattered society. Interviewers asked about democracy and new elections and a free media. I scoffed and came off as a dick because I dismissed those concerns as foolish and irrelevant; how could you hold elections in a country whose population was listed as "estimated," where people weren't sure of their birth dates, where streets didn't have names and houses didn't have numbers? How could anyone campaign in a place awash with automatic weapons, a place devoid of law, order, or common decency, where a ten-year-old kid—I saw him—could walk into the street and shoot innocent people to death just for fun and have no one act in response because they were afraid and/or didn't care?

Who cares about a free press when you can't afford to buy a newspaper or a television set? Who cares about freedom of speech when you don't know whether you're going to live or die, or whether your wife will make it back from the market without getting raped? Law and order are the first thing you need for society to exist. Everything else is a luxury.

Interviewers asked about business. What, they wanted to know, would be the economy of the New Afghanistan, as they were calling it? As a failed state, Afghanistan didn't even have a central currency system. Two rival warlords printed different sets of afghani notes in Russia at whim. They looked the same, but one was bluish green whereas the other was greenish blue; since one was considered worth twice as much as the other, a common method of cheating involved giving change in the "wrong" notes.

In 2000 and 2001 the Taliban had agreed to crack down on opium production; in exchange the United States made the payroll of the Taliban government. (You shouldn't believe this. It's outlandish. But look it up! It's true.) That left a nation with one hundred percent unemployment. Pomegranate exports were its top economic activity. Here's how fucked up Afghanistan was: *they couldn't even make carpets anymore*. Business? How on earth was Afghanistan going to establish business? You can't have capitalism unless you have a strong nation-state to enforce rules and regulations and laws to make sure that contracts have effect. In Afghanistan, the only law was that the person with the biggest weapons and the best aim tended to prevail. Hardly a place to start building factories and opening stores.

It was hard not to scoff when the free press question came up. Censorship isn't a big problem when there's no media whatsoever. No newspapers. No radio. No TV. It should be noted, however, that a nascent market for Pakistani and Indian pornography emerged at the Taloqan bazaar six days after the Taliban withdrawal. Number one at the box office: *Thounders Boobs*.

Afghanistan in the fall of 2001: there was nothing. No business, no jobs. No paved roads, almost no cars. No electricity, no running water, no telephones, cellular or otherwise. No police, no government, not even mosques. I was accustomed to Muslim countries like Pakistan, where people stop what they're doing to pray several times a day and the call to prayer fills the sky. Not so in northern Afghanistan. Every institution had been destroyed by decades of war. Families left bereft, headed by impoverished widows, many of them victims of rape. Government, the idea of the nation-state, replaced by might-makes-right warlordism. Infrastructure—bridges, roads, tunnels, buildings, pipes, wires—gone. There was hardly any food, though this began to change after the U.S. invasion. Bags of rice, marked "USAID—Not for Resale," were delivered to the border, seized by warlord militias, and sold at local bazaars. I was often asked about reports that the U.S. Air Force was dropping millions of military "meals ready to eat" to feed the starving people of Afghanistan. Had I seen them? Were the people grateful? No, I never did. I asked Afghans about them, but nobody knew what I was talking about. Later I heard that some of the MREs destined for poor Afghans had fallen near Kabul and been bogarted by the warlords.

All that was left of Afghanistan was the Afghan people themselves. The slow, the meek, the generous, the honest, the disloyal—these had died or been killed. Those who remained were brilliant, hardworking liars. Men and women who would do and say anything to survive and were impossible to befriend, unless you did, in which case they would give you anything, even their lives. They were infuriating and scheming and brave and cowardly and warm and fascinating. Lois from the *Post* told me that before arriving in Taloqan from Shah Massoud's final headquarters at Khwaja Bahauddin, she offhandedly mentioned to some villagers that she would love a proper house to stay in—as opposed to camping outdoors. Six hours later, she recounted, she got her wish: a new mudbrick house, with a real thatched roof, even a *hamam* with drainage. "There were even window curtains," she said.

The Afghan people, I thought in 2001, are going to be fine. All they need to rebuild their country is help with infrastructure—and then to be left alone.

ONE: THE BEGINNING OF THE END

We took our eye off the ball. And not to mention that we are still spending $10 billion a month when [the Iraqis] have a $79 billion surplus, at a time when we are in great distress here at home . . . We took our eye off Afghanistan. We took our eye off the folks who perpetrated 9/11. They are still sending out videotapes.

—Barack Obama, during a presidential debate against John McCain on September 27, 2008

The more troops you bring the more troubles you will have here.

—Zamir Kabulov, Soviet ambassador to Afghanistan and press attaché in Kabul from 1983 to 1987, September 13, 2009

It should have come as little surprise, when Barack Obama took office in January 2009, that he would expand and prolong the war against Afghanistan.

Throughout the 2008 campaign, Obama echoed John Kerry's 2004 formulation of the Iraq War as "the wrong war in the wrong place at the wrong time." Afghanistan, both by implication and declaration, was the war the United States ought to have been fighting after the September 11, 2001, attacks: "Let me be clear," Obama said two months into his presidency: "Al Qaeda and its allies—the terrorists who planned and supported the 9/11 attacks—are in Pakistan and Afghanistan. Multiple intelligence estimates have warned that Al Qaeda is actively planning attacks on the U.S. homeland from its safe haven in Pakistan. And if the Afghan government falls to the Taliban—or allows Al Qaeda to go unchallenged—that country will again be a base for terrorists who want to kill as many of our people as they possibly can."

In 2002, George W. Bush transferred tens of thousands of troops and attendant military support personnel and materiel from Afghanistan—then considered largely in the mopping-up stage—to Iraq. In 2009, Obama reversed Bush, transferring forty thousand soldiers back to Afghanistan. Afghanistan became "Obama's War," as the headlines called it.

But the mood of the public had changed. Americans were tired of perpetual war. They were worried about rising unemployment and falling wages. They saw their new president turning away from the problems they cared about—no jobs—in order to focus on the war in Afghanistan, a war that would soon become the longest in American history. And they didn't like what they saw. Seven out of ten Americans had favored the war in 2001. By 2009, a third of the public had changed their minds.

So Obama set a deadline. U.S. troops would begin leaving Afghanistan in July 2011. Paradoxically it was part of his Afghan "surge" strategy. Go in fast, go in hard, "degrade" the Taliban resistance, gain time to train the Afghan national army and police so they could take over after the Americans leave.

America's war against Afghanistan had been declared "over soon" before. Several times. In early 2002, after Karzai assumed the presidency. In 2003, when Iraq became the Pentagon's Job One. In 2005, after parliamentary elections (never mind the widespread fraud). In 2009, after Karzai was sort-of-reelected (same note re: fraud).

This time, however, I believed it. Not because Obama was saying it and not Bush, but because Obama didn't have a reasonable alternative. The post-2008 depression was costing half a million American jobs a month. Largely because of the "global war on terror" (i.e., Iraq and Afghanistan), the federal budget was stretched close to its breaking point, with the deficit soaring to a shocking 13 percent of gross domestic product. (This was the highest level since 1943, the peak of World War II production.) The war was an expensive, unpopular distraction. It had to be wound down.

The "surge"? I assumed that that was for propaganda purposes, for Obama to give himself political coverage when critics accused him and the Democrats of "cutting and running" in the face of radical Islam.

As the Obama administration began its second year, I wondered how things had changed in Afghanistan since my ill-fated trip there in 2001. Media reports had become sporadic, sketchy, and unreliable, so frequently failing to jibe with verifiable facts that I eventually stopped believing any of them. They were also few and far between. Newspapers and broadcast outlets, devastated by the Internet revolution as well as a general economic downturn that had reduced ad dollars throughout the 2000s, sent their war correspondents to Iraq if they didn't fire them outright.

I made friends in 2001 who, in other situations, would have proven useful contacts during my return. But Afghanistan's communications infrastructure, nonexistent at the time, had not allowed for the usual exchange of street addresses, much less phone numbers or email. "I'd like to keep in touch," I told my fixer as we'd said goodbye. He shrugged. I said it out loud: "No mail . . . no phone . . . how?" The cast of characters that had defined my life during those crazy three weeks in 2001 faded from my life. Afghanistan went dark.

After 2001 the publication of my books about the region had prompted many Westerners and Afghans to get in touch with me in order to discuss the state of the nation. Their reports had the feel of that hoary story about blind people feeling an elephant. They were often conflicting: some U.S. soldiers told me Afghanistan was a disaster, that nothing but nothing had been rebuilt and that the Afghans hated "us" (i.e., Americans), while others claimed that lots of "good things" were getting done that the liberal media weren't bothering to report due to its partisan agenda.

Mainstream sources, limited as they were, reported that Afghanistan was relatively stable in 2002, 2003, and 2004. Security was far from assured, but it wasn't a "hot" war. But the people I talked to—Afghan refugees who emailed me from the West, NGO workers, U.S. and foreign occupation soldiers—told a different story. They said Afghans were appalled at the utter lack of public infrastructure reconstruction: roads, schools, hospitals, homeless shelters. They were disgusted by the fact that the United States had reinstalled the hated warlords whose depravity and corruption had fueled the rise of the Taliban in the mid-1990s. They were frightened at the complete lack of central government control outside the major cities of Kabul, Mazar-i-Sharif, Herat, and Kandahar. Afghanistan, they said, was a war that was rapidly becoming "Arabized." Tactics such as suicide bombings and IEDs, previously unknown there, were being adapted and imported by the Taliban, their neo-Taliban successors, and other anti-Karzai groups.

By 2005, NGO workers, American soldiers, and Afghan contacts were telling me that insufficient—actually, a total lack of—reconstruction was the secondmost complaint about the American troop presence. (The foremost gripe was the presence itself. As far as I can tell, there has never been a military occupation that was welcomed by the majority of the population of any country, at least not for long.) As I had written in a 2001 report for *The Village Voice*, you only get one chance to make a good first impression—and the United States had blown it. Assuming it had been possible to get Afghans to forget about the devastating, callous air campaign that had blown up so many wedding parties that the tragedies became a sick joke of a cliché, the one thing "we" could have done to have improved "our" popularity with the Afghans would have been to have fulfilled Bush's promise of a Marshall Plan for Afghanistan.

Afghans view the United States as something between man and god: incomprehensively rich, organizationally sophisticated, and capable of building a new country from the ground up with one hand tied behind its back. Afghans expected instant results—if not instant, close to it. What they got instead was jack shit. By 2005, *The New York Times* was reporting that the United States had not so much as slapped two bricks together in four years. It hadn't paved an inch of roadway. There were explanations for this, some reasonable, most not, all involving bureaucracy and unfamiliarity with culture and politics in Afghanistan, the security situation, and so on; the Afghans weren't interested in anything other than results.

In 2007 I had gone to Tajikistan to research a feature story about Lake Sarez. Lake Sarez was formed a century ago when an earthquake triggered a landslide that blocked the Murgab River in the high Pamir mountains in central Tajikistan. Glacier melt caused by global warming has caused the water level to rise, imperiling the natural dam. If and when the dam breaks, computer models predict, a wall of water eight hundred feet high will cascade down the Murgab River valley and through a succession of other canyons and rivers until it peters out a thousand miles away in the deserts of Uzbekistan, leaving one to five million people dead and 90 percent of the arable land in Central Asia silted and barren.

My 2007 journey took me along the Pyanj River, which separates Tajikistan and Afghanistan. There were a few signs of development on the Afghan side: a special trade zone where Tajiks could shop for Afghan goods and a four-star hotel booked up by NGO workers, mostly Doctors Without Borders (but never without reservations, evidently). For the most part, however, it didn't seem like much had changed. At night there were still lights only on the Tajik side. Women, when they appeared in public, told the story: on the Tajik side, they wore traditional dresses with floral prints or tight Western miniskirts and white blouses; Afghans were still in their burqas.

I wanted to go back. I wanted to find out what had changed, what was better, worse, how Afghans were faring under the occupation. More than anything, I wanted to shed light on the Big Question No One Ever Wants to Think About, at least not in the United States: Why do "we" (the U.S. government and military, and by extension people) keep getting into this sort of thing? Why are we mired in an economy based on endless war and a culture of mindless militarism? Whether you view the quagmires of Vietnam and Afghanistan as messes we somehow got stuck in, or you consider them essential elements of an aggressive neo-colonialist foreign policy, why do we do it? We never win. We pay a terrible price. Yet we keep sending tens of thousands of men and women to fight and kill and die or come back wrecked. We keep spending insane portions of national treasure on these military misadventures. Why? At this writing we spend 54 percent of the federal budget on "defense." Seventeen percent is debt service on old wars. One out of six tax dollars goes to paying debt for wars we've already lost!

Perhaps by examining the history of and situation in one of America's little wars, its most recent, it is possible to dissect not only what went wrong there but what is wrong with our way of looking at the world, our way of life . . . ourselves.

I wanted to see the places American and other Western reporters rarely if ever go. Everyone flew in and out of Kabul. A few intrepid souls covered the fighting along the eastern border with Pakistan, and in the south, especially in Helmand province, where U.S. forces had been fighting Taliban forces for several years. But no one ever went to the north, center, or west of the country. Surely there was a story there. Even if nothing much was going on, I still wanted to find out how the American occupation had impacted the lives of ordinary people.

I also wanted to file reports in a way that no one had ever done before: in real-time cartoon blogs.

Comics journalism, also called "comix journalism," has been around since even before Bill Mauldin's *Willie and Joe* cartoons from World War II. Comics journalism in its modern form was created by Joe Sacco. A Maltese American cartoonist, Sacco went to the Balkans in the mid-1990s, came back home, and drew slice-of-life narrative comics about what he saw. In 2000 he published his first collection of war comics, *Safe Area Goražde: The War in Eastern Bosnia, 1992–1995.* His *Palestine,* about his time on the occupied West Bank, came out a year later. When I did *To Afghanistan and Back,* I followed the same template: go, take notes and photos, come home, compile, draw comics. Later notables in the field, such as David Axe and Guy Delisle, do it the same way.

There are practical reasons for the see-it-draw-it-later approach, not the least of which is the fact that most cartoonists prefer a comfortable, quiet place to draw and that a little hindsight helps them figure out what is most interesting to readers. On the other hand, this approach sacrifices immediacy. Whether they work in prose or on camera, most war correspondents file within hours of researching a story. Why not a cartoonist?

The blogging explosion inspired me to try to file a blog in comics form every single day from Afghanistan. I solved one impediment right away: time. When you're traveling vast distances every day in a place that's dangerous, hot, and uncomfortable, it's hard to find the time or energy to spend four to six hours drawing and coloring cartoons every day. The solution, I decided, was simplicity. One of my favorite cartoonists is Jeffrey Smith. He bangs out his cartoons in a no-nonsense sketch style. I would do the same. No fussy lines, not even a ruler. I'd use the same stripped-down drawing style I usually use on the rough drawings I send to editors for approval before I draw the final product. To keep myself focused mentally on the idea rather than the form, I would leave my usual Bristol board at home and draw on plain old photocopy paper. No customized Rapidograph pens; they jam and leak and explode. Just a black ballpoint pen would be fine. I should be able to draw a page or two an hour.

Delivery would be difficult. From what I could gather from news accounts, the communications infrastructure in Afghanistan was still terrible to nonexistent. There might be a few cybercafés in Kabul, but I planned to spend most of my time in rural areas. There'd be no power or phones. I'd have to take a portable flatbed scanner as well as a laptop. Since my MacBook Pro held a charge for at most two hours, I'd need extra batteries. But those were one hundred twenty dollars each. And they're heavy. So I'd also need solar panels and a battery cell, which I could use to recharge the laptop.

Once a cartoon was loaded onto the laptop and processed into an emailable format, it would need to be sent to a friend in the States who would then post it to my blog and any client newspapers I managed to scare up. Fortunately things had improved since '01, when I was forced to use dial-up service at 2400 bps on an ancient Iridium satellite phone that dropped most of the calls halfway through. A company in Tennessee agreed to rent me a satellite modem called a BGAN that promised direct Internet connection speeds comparable to digital cable.

But how would I get there? Afghanistan was an expensive destination. Airfare was the least of the challenge; as I'd learned in 2001, Afghan rates for transport and housing are nothing short of extortion. They're not bluffing. Afghans will turn you away rather than take fifty bucks for a day of driving. This in a country with one hundred percent unemployment and an average wage (for the few who get one) of twenty dollars a month.

The route I wanted to take would add to the problems and thus the costs: across the north via Mazar and Maimana to Herat, then south to the western desert along the border with Iran, exiting via Iran. (The northern route would allow me to cover areas rarely seen by Western journalists.) Although Iran and the United States still don't have diplomatic relations, American nationals can ostensibly obtain tourist visas—but what I wanted to do would be unusual even by rarefied American-tourist-in-Iran standards. I would be traveling independently and would be entering through a border that Iran viewed with suspicion since it was used by smugglers, terrorists, arms dealers, drug traffickers, and similar dodgy sorts. No American citizen had been granted a visa to enter Iran from Afghanistan since the 1979 Islamic Revolution. If that door was to be pried open, it would occur only following the judicious application of money.

All told, I figured it would cost about thirty to forty thousand dollars to go to Afghanistan for a month. In the 1990s and early 2000s, writers pitched this sort of trip to magazines. But in 2010, magazines were folding right and left, editors being laid off daily. Print media was entering the tenth year of a devastating economic tailspin. No one was interested in paying for war correspondency.

In 2001, I had been able to cobble together a budget between an AM talk radio station in L.A. and the once eminent and rabble-rousing *Village Voice*. It was tougher in 2010. I sent queries to alternative weekly newspapers across the country, figuring I might be able to get one or two dozen of them to split the cost. I contacted more than a hundred of them. Not one replied. The situation wasn't much better at the radio and TV outlets I approached. Their ad revenues had been savaged and they were suffering their own wounds in the losing battle against the digital revolution. I didn't know what to do.

I mentioned my frustration to my friends. One colleague and long-time friend, the cartoonist and essayist Stephanie McMillan, mentioned that she had successfully raised more than five thousand dollars through a website, Kickstarter, to finance the printing and distribution of a children's book she had illustrated for the environmental writer Derrick Jensen. Typically, in exchange for rewards like a free book or original artwork, people who want to see a project realized pledge a sum they're willing to pay. The project creator gets the money only if the target amount is raised. "Try Kickstarter," she urged. "It couldn't hurt."

I posted the same pitch I had sent to the editors, along with a short video. I asked backers for a total of $25,000 and gave myself ninety days to raise the money.

Three months later, I had pledges from two hundred eleven supporters—many of whom had previously been unfamiliar with my work—for a total of $26,000. I didn't promise them much: just the satisfaction of contributing to an attempt to "find out the truth about Afghanistan," regular updates, and, if it worked out, a copy of this book.

Who needs a news organization? If you have support and a way to reach your supporters, you can find everything you need: the laptop, the solar panels, the satellite phone. Sure, nobody's really going to pay a ransom if you get kidnapped. But maybe that will reduce your chances of getting kidnapped in the first place.

I was going to Afghanistan.

One can travel alone, and I enjoy it sometimes, but I have found that a good traveling companion can make the difference between life and death in a conflict zone. An extra brain can generate an idea that would never have occurred to you. Having someone familiar around soothes you during times of stress. So I asked myself who among my friends would (a) be insane enough to want to go to U.S.-occupied Afghanistan during the full throes of an insurgency and (b) fun enough

I HAVE 3 MAIN MISSIONS. FIRST: FIND JOVID.

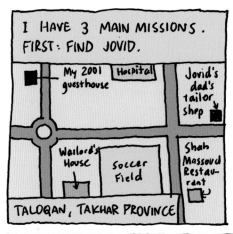

TALOQAN, TAKHAR PROVINCE

My 2001 guesthouse

Hospital

Jovid's dad's tailor shop

Warlord's House

Soccer Field

Shah Massoud Restaurant

JOVID WAS MY FIXER. HE'S 33 NOW. IF HE'S STILL ALIVE.

HE STINKS!

TRUE. BUT HE'S HONEST. HE HASN'T LIED TO US.

A FIXER MAKES THINGS HAPPEN. HE TRANSLATES. HE FINDS PLACES TO STAY. HE GETS THINGS. HE PROTECTS YOU.

I WORRY ABOUT JOVID. HE'S WEAK. HE'S HONEST. HE'S NICE. HE GOT ME OUT IN '01, WHEN SOLDIERS CAME LOOKING TO KILL ME.

Graying Hair

MY FATHER WANTED ME TO JOIN A MILITIA. I REFUSED.

Age 24

I ASSUME HE STILL LIVES IN TALOQAN. I'M SURE HIS FAMILY STILL DOES. IT'S NOT LIKE IT'S EASY TO PACK UP AND GO. I WANT TO VISIT THEM, HIRE ONE OR MORE OF THEM TO GET US TO MAZAR-I-SHARIF, PUT SOME MONEY IN THEIR POCKETS.

PASSPORT

THE TALIBAN HAVE TAKEN TALOQAN 3 TIMES IN THE LAST FEW YEARS. SO I DON'T KNOW WHO I'LL FIND IN CHARGE.

THEN I HAVE TO FIND THE PIPELINE.

THE TRANS-AFGHANISTAN PIPELINE IS, DEPENDING ON WHOM YOU ASK, A HOAX, A FACT, A CONSPIRACY, A MIRAGE, A DREAM. TAP WAS CONCEIVED IN THE MID-1990s AS A "NEW SILK ROAD" THAT WOULD CARRY OIL AND NATURAL GAS FROM THE LANDLOCKED CASPIAN SEA OIL WELLS OF KAZAKHSTAN AND TURKMENISTAN TO THE ARABIAN SEA CITY OF MULTAN, PAKISTAN.

Proposed Route of Oil and Gas Pipeline

VIA AFGHANISTAN.

ASIDE FROM A BRIEF MENTION IN MICHAEL MOORE'S "FAHRENHEIT 911," FEW MAINSTREAM MEDIA HAVE MENTIONED THE PROJECT.

IT'S JUST A LOONY LEFT **CONSPIRACY THEORY.**

BUT FOREIGN NEWS REPORTS SAY THE PIPELINE IS BEING BUILT. NOW. NORTH OF HERAT, IN NORTHWESTERN AFGHANISTAN. IS IT TRUE? THERE'S ONLY ONE WAY TO FIND OUT FOR SURE: GO SEE IT FOR MYSELF.

FIRST WE FIND PIPELINE WORKERS. WHICH MEANS: FAKE BRITISH PUB.

IN HERAT, RIGHT?

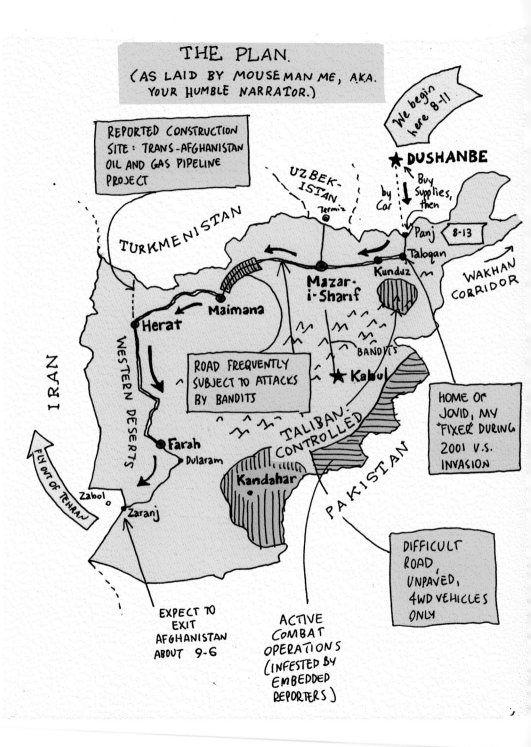

PLANNING FOR A TRIP TO AFGHANISTAN INVOLVES A LOT OF NEGATIVES.

YOU WANT TO AVOID GETTING BLOWN UP BY AN I.E.D.

WHICH RULES OUT THE EASTERN AND SOUTHERN PARTS OF THE COUNTRY.

YOU DON'T WANT TO BE AN OBVIOUS TARGET.

SO YOU STAY AWAY FROM U.S. TROOPS AND NGO PERSONNEL.

YOU WANT TO STAY AWAY FROM BANDITS.

SO YOU DON'T FLY INTO KABUL AND DRIVE THE ROAD TO MAZAR-I-SHARIF.

THERE ARE ALSO NEGATIVES OF EMPHASIS.

40 MILLION NEWS ACCOUNTS FROM THE EAST AND THE SOUTH — DOESN'T ANYONE EVER GO TO THE NORTH OR THE WEST?

WHICH CAN CAUSE CONFUSION.

SO YOU'RE WITH THE TROOPS.

SO YOU'LL BE IN KABUL.

SO YOU'RE FRIENDS WITH THE "THREE CUPS OF TEA" GUY.

NO — I'LL BE INDEPENDENT.

NEVER. THE STORY IS ALL OUTSIDE KABUL.

I SHOULD GO AWAY BEFORE I SAY NO AGAIN.

PREPARATION FOR THE JOURNEY FOCUSED ON 3 MAIN ISSUES:

TRAVELING COMPANION

I.E., THE GUY WHO SAVES YOU — OR GETS YOU KILLED!

FINANCING

WAR ZONE GUIDES
Afghanistan on $500 a day

VISAS

2   23

TOTALITARIAN REPUBLIC OF STANISTAN

MY FIRST CHOICE OF TRAVELING COMPADRE WAS COLE SMITHEY, THE FILM CRITIC. HE HAS NERVES OF STEEL.

WHEN THE TALIBAN THREATENED TO EXECUTE COLE AND ME IN KASHMIR IN 1999, HE SLEPT THROUGH IT.

BUT COLE COULDN'T GO.

SO I ASKED MATT BORS. MATT IS A FELLOW POLITICAL CARTOONIST. AND A FRIEND. HE'S 27.

I'M IN!

PORTLAND, OR

AUGUST? DURING THE HOTTEST TIME OF THE YEAR? DURING THE CRUNCH TIME OF THE ENTIRE WAR? DURING RAMADAN? **AWESOME.**

JUST THE RIGHT ATTITUDE.

HOW MUCH TRAVEL HAVE YOU DONE?

BASICALLY, NOT THAT MUCH.

ABROAD?   NONE.

to hang out with for a whole month in a country where watching TV wouldn't be an option.

I called Matt Bors. At twenty-seven he was two decades younger than I am, yet we always seem to be on the same page. He's a low-key guy, lives in Portland though like me he grew up in Ohio, a fellow political cartoonist, very smart. He has the kind of eyes that make you feel like you're being scanned and will be summarily rejected and disposed of should you come up wanting in some regard. When he calls, his first utterance will likely be a deadpan "Hey."

We met in earnest when I worked at United Media as editor of acquisitions; I signed up his cartoons for national syndication, which made him the youngest syndicated political cartoonist in the country. We talk often, both of us clicking away on our computers, Photoshopping our cartoons at the same time, as we mock the state of the editorial cartooning profession and contemporary politics.

Matt was instantly excited. However, he had never left the United States before. Not Mexico. Not Canada. He didn't even have a passport. Maybe I was crazy, but I viewed Bors's lack of travel experience as a plus. The last experienced traveler I had teamed up with in Central Asia had managed to get himself arrested at the Bishkek airport—and that was after he split open his skull on the diving board at the hotel in Ashkhabat while showing off for girls—while the newbies always managed to muddle through. I figured Bors would do fine. Except, of course, for the diarrhea.

HOLIDAY IN THE SUN: TRAVEL PLANNING FOR AFGHANISTAN
MAY 13, 2010

How are things going in Afghanistan? The best way to find out is to go see for yourself. I'm doing that this August.

THE CARTOONING COMMUNITY IS SMALL. (AND, THANKS TO NEWSPAPER BUDGET CUTS, GETTING SMALLER.) SO WORD GOT OUT QUICKLY THAT MATT BORS AND I WERE PLANNING TO GO TO AFGHANISTAN.

Steven L. Cloud Cartoonist, "Boy on a Stick and Slither", 37

I **REALLY** WANT TO GO ON THIS TRIP. I ONLY FEEL REALLY ALIVE WHEN I'M TRAVELING.

Awesome Beard

OLDE TOWNE BAR

STEVEN WENT ON A CRAZY TRANS-ASIA EASTERN-EUROPE-TO-MONGOLIA CHARITY RALLY VIA RUSSIA AND KAZAKHSTAN.

I DIDN'T KNOW STEVEN VERY WELL. BUT HE'D ALWAYS STRUCK ME AS INTELLIGENT, STEADY, AND A GO-GETTER. AN EXTRA SMART 3RD MAN COULDN'T HURT.

HE'S COOL.

I'D FEEL BETTER IF HE WENT WITH YOU.

HOW COOL?

MY INSTINCTS PROVED CORRECT. WHEN THE VISA PROCESS TURNED UGLY, STEVEN ROSE TO THE OCCASION.

BEWARE THE RULE OF THREE.

THE MORE, THE MERRIER.

SO THE TEAM WAS FINAL: TRES AMIGOS!

TED RALL
AGE: 47
JOB: CARTOONIST

AS: "The Idiot Who Thought This Up"

STEVEN CLOUD
AGE: 37
JOB: CARTOONIST

AS: "Mr. Calm"

MATT BORS
AGE: 27
JOB: CARTOONIST

AS: "The Ingenue"

NEVER EVEN WENT TO MEXICO!

You can tell a lot even before you go. I'm in the planning stages: reserving flights, applying for visas, buying equipment.

"Whatever you do," a friend emailed me from Kabul, "don't fly into the Kabul airport." He wasn't worried that my flight would get shot down by one of Reagan's leftover Stinger missiles—although there's a risk of that. (In order to improve the odds, pilots corkscrew in and out.)

His concern is corrupt cops. "[Afghan president Hamid] Karzai's policemen are crazy," my normally taciturn buddy, who works for an NGO, elaborated. "They'll hold you up at gunpoint right in the airport."

One option is to hitch a flight on a military transport to the former Soviet airbase north of town at Bagram, now a U.S. torture facility being expanded by the Obama administration in order to accommodate detainees being transferred from Guantánamo. But I'm an old-fashioned journalist. War reporters shouldn't tag along with soldiers.

So I'm not flying into Kabul. Which works out, since getting to my destination—Taloqan, in Takhar province near the Tajik border—would have required traveling north toward Mazar-i-Sharif from Kabul. Among the highlights of the Kabul–Mazar road are landslides and a trek through the pockmarked Soviet-era Salang Tunnel. It also offers an assortment of thugs both political (Taliban) and apolitical (bandits).

To avoid corrupt airport cops and the dicey north-south highway, I'll fly into Dushanbe, the capital of Afghanistan's northern neighbor, Tajikistan. This means spending an extra eight hundred dollars on airfare, not to mention chancing travel on one of Tajikistan Airlines' aging Tupolev 154s. It takes a full day to drive from Dushanbe to the Afghan border on mostly unpaved roads.

But I'll be stuck in Dushanbe for two or three days waiting for government permits. You can't travel to the special "security zone" along the border with Afghanistan without a permission document issued by the Tajik Ministry of Foreign Affairs. When I met the minister in 2001, I asked him whether treating the hundred-kilometer zone like a no-man's-land sent an unfriendly message to the Afghans. He laughed. "Afghanistan," he said, "is our very difficult neighbor. If they behave better, so will we." The policy remains in place.

No journalist operating in a war zone is safe without a fixer. Things you can easily do yourself back home can be impossible in the fourth world. A fixer makes things happen: government permits, cars and drivers, places to stay. I've accumulated a set of fixers throughout Central and South Asia over the years.

But it's hard to arrange a fixer in advance in Afghanistan. There's hardly any mail, telephone service, or electricity outside Kabul, much less email. I'll probably have to just show up, then hire people as I travel.

Nevertheless, I contacted another Kabul-based Friend of Rall about lining up fixers for the regions I plan to visit: Takhar, which I mentioned above, Kunduz, then northern Afghanistan en route to and around Herat (near the Turkmen and Iranian borders), and finally Nimruz province.

There's heavy fighting in Kunduz. The Taliban recently beheaded four guards working for U.S. forces near Herat. In Zaranj, the provincial capital of Nimruz, suicide bombers just took out the governor's compound.

"No one wants to go where you're going," my friend informed me.

The average salary in Afghanistan is thirty dollars per month.

"I pay one hundred fifty a day," I replied.

"I know a guy. But he's a whiner. He'll complain about it the whole time. And you'll have to promise a death bonus to his wife if something happens."

Communications are a challenge. I want to file a daily cartoon blog. I can scan a drawn cartoon into my laptop, assuming it doesn't get stolen by some greedy border guard. But how will I access the Internet?

I can rent a satellite phone and use dial-up. It won't be fast; at 9600 bps it takes an hour to send one simple black-and-white cartoon. And it won't be easy. Dial-up lines drop. In 2001, when I paid seven dollars a minute for satellite service, I cried when that happened. The search for power will be endless. Solar panels, car batteries, renting a generator for an hour, whatever it takes to feed greedy phones and laptops.

I'm not complaining. I'm just saying.

Afghans are allowed to complain. They live there.

Of course, the biggest inconvenience is danger.

Everyone worries about me. "Keep your head down." "Come back alive." "Don't get killed."

They're sweet and loving sentiments. But they're also kind of funny. Most of my friends still think of Afghanistan as the Good War, the one that had something—they're not sure what—to do with 9/11. They think we're there to help the Afghans. They think the carnage is in Iraq; actually, it's more dangerous for U.S. troops in Afghanistan.

If the Afghanistan War is going so well, why is everyone so worried?

I spent the next few months planning the trip. Mostly this involved visa applications and buying and renting supplies. I began letting my beard grow. In 2001 the Taliban were strictly enforcing their requirement that men's facial hair be at least the size of a fist clenched under the chin, wild and untrimmed, in areas they controlled. On more than one occasion I argued with Talibs about this stricture, noting that it's

not in the Koran. The beard requirement is, however, in the Sunnah.*
But the Sunnah does not specify *whose* fist should be used to measure
a beard. "It could be a small child's fist," I said. "A fetus's, even."
Though hilarious, this was a deadly serious topic of conversation. Men
have been beaten and even shot for coming up short in the facial hair
department. I was determined to avoid the issue by having a beard
worthy of any fist the Taliban chose to put up.

It's easy to get a visa for a country your country is occupying. Because the security situation might explode at a moment's notice and
you can't just show up at an international border crossing in the middle
of a desert without a visa, however, prudence also required applying for
entry permits to every neighboring country to which we might need to
flee before we left for the States. For example, I spent hundreds of dollars
for a visa to Uzbekistan, even though I had no plans to go there and
could only use it as an exit from one Afghan city: Mazar-i-Sharif. I
planned to enter Afghanistan via Tajikistan, as in 2001. What if things
got hairy and I had to immediately hightail it back to the border? That
contingency required a double-entry visa. We'd also need a just-in-case
visa for Turkmenistan—but those had become virtually impossible† to
obtain after the recent death of President Saparmurat "Turkmenbashi"
Niyazov.

I would also need a fixer. I had no way of reaching Jovid, who had
taken such good care of me in 2001, so—riding the optimism of my
Kickstarter success—I tried to look for an Afghan fixer online. But
that proved just as impossible as it would have been nine years earlier.
Google searches revealed a few "logistics" companies based in Kabul

---

* In Sunni Islam, the Sunnah is a collection of narrations and approvals about the
deeds, sayings, habits, and beliefs of the Prophet Muhammad. Believers turn to the
Sunnah for answers to questions about behavior relative to friends, family members,
and government officials.

† Code for "requires bigger bribe than usual."

IT'S IMPOSSIBLE TO EXPLAIN IN WORDS — OR WORDS WITH PICTURES — HOW ONEROUS, HOW AWFUL, HOW MUCH OF A COLOSSAL PAIN IN THE BUTT IT WAS TO OBTAIN THE VISAS FOR THIS TRIP TO AFGHANISTAN. IMPOSSIBLE. BUT LET'S TRY:

AFGHANISTAN IS A BREEZE. A FORM, SOME PASSPORT PHOTOS, AND A FEE — AND YOU'RE IN.

Starting to Grow a Beard to Prepare

THE AFGHAN CONSULATE IS NEW TO THE BUILDING. THEY CAN'T WORK THE BUZZER.

THEY'RE HAPPY TO TAKE YOUR MONEY.

BUT WE NEEDED VISAS FOR 4 OTHER COUNTRIES: TAJIKISTAN, UZBEKISTAN, TURKMENISTAN, AND IRAN.

TAJIKISTAN, AS OUR POINT OF ENTRY INTO AFGHANISTAN.

WE GOT A DOUBLE-ENTRY VISA SO WE COULD GET BACK OUT IF NEED BE.

UZBEKISTAN, AS A BACKUP PLAN. A VERY SPECIFIC BACKUP. IF SOMETHING WENT WRONG IN MAZAR-I-SHARIF, WE COULD USE THE "FRIENDSHIP BRIDGE"* TO CROSS THE SHORT UZBEK-AFGHAN BORDER.

UZ

TERMIZ

Amu   Darya

AFG

MAZAR-I-SHARIF

* THE USSR INVADED AFGHAN-ISTAN VIA THIS BRIDGE.

TURKMENISTAN, AS ANOTHER BACK-UP PLAN: IN CASE THE BORDER WITH IRAN GOT CLOSED. OR IF THINGS TURNED UGLY DURING OUR NORTHERN LEG.

TURKMENISTAN

M

Maimana

HERAT

OUR PLANNED POINT OF EGRESS WAS IRAN.

THANK YOU FOR CALLING IRANIAN INTERESTS SECTION OF EMBASSY OF PAKISTAN. GOODBYE. (CLICK)

WT?

Panel 1: IRAN SEEMED DETERMINED TO TAKE OUT ITS FURY OVER U.S. TRADE SANCTIONS AGAINST ME PERSONALLY — BY DRIVING ME CRAZY.

THE IRANIAN INTERESTS SECTION OF THE PAKISTANI EMBASSY IN D.C. SAYS I HAVE TO APPLY AT THE U.N. MISSION IN NYC BECAUSE I'M A JOURNALIST.

Panel 2: BUT THE N.Y. OFFICE SAYS THAT BECAUSE I WON'T BE DOING JOURNALISTIC WORK IN IRAN, I HAVE TO GO THROUGH D.C., SO I DO. BUT:

MAY

"REJECTED. MINORS UNDER 18 NEED PARENTS' PERMISSION"?!?

Panel 3: FINALLY, I FIND THE SAME FIXERS NPR REPORTERS USE IN TEHRAN. THEY DROP OFF YOUR VISA APPLICATION RIGHT AT THE MINISTRY OF FOREIGN AFFAIRS. WHERE IT DISAPPEARS FOREVER.

WHAT DO YOU MEAN, I NEVER APPLIED? YOU IDIOTS ALREADY TOLD ME IT WAS *APPROVED*!!

JULY

Received

Panel 4: WHERE I HAVE FAILED, STEVEN SUCCEEDS.

YOU GET THE APPROVAL CODE FROM AN IRANIAN TOUR AGENCY AND USE THAT TO APPLY IN D.C. D.C. NEEDS OUR BANK STATEMENTS TOO. THE AGENCY WANTS 3,000 EUROS.

I JUST WIRED IT TO THEM.

COOL!

WE'RE ALL SET.

that specialized in providing armored vehicles and scary gunmen to journalists and businesspeople who want to get in and out of the country with as many of their limbs still attached as possible and are willing to pay any price for that assurance. Aside from not wanting to isolate myself from the Afghans—after all, talking to Afghans was the purpose of the trip—I disapprove of this approach to security. The diciest situations I've found myself in in Central and South Asia usually have come about because I was too conspicuous. Being discreet, in my experience, is always best.

Ideally, you want to look as much like a local as you possibly can. Even if your looks are distinctly nonlocal—and that's not usually a problem in Central Asia, where there are lots of Caucasian-looking people—the right clothes can go a really long way. In Iran and Turkmenistan, for example, men between the ages of thirty and sixty tend to wear the same crappy gray V-neck sweaters. Pick up one of those things at the local bazaar for five bucks, and it buys you an extra few minutes at a checkpoint. That can save your life. Or at least a few dollars in bribes.

Every signifier that makes you look different increases your risk of detection. If they're looking for you, they're going to find you. But mostly they're not looking for you. What happens to Westerners is that they drive around in flashy cars, surrounded by obnoxious security personnel, and stay in expensive safehouses and four-star hotels. It usually doesn't take very long before some enterprising villain sees them as an opportunity and tries to kidnap them or rob them or worse. So I always make an effort to localize myself as much as possible. I prefer to stay with local families, because even though they will tell everyone in the neighborhood that you are staying there, local codes of hospitality require them to take good care of you and, if need be, even to protect you with their own lives.

I thought maybe I could tap my informal network of fixers, grown over the course of eight trips to Central Asia, for referrals to people in Afghanistan. My Uzbek and Tajik fixers were eager to help as far as they could—but their knowledge of the situation stopped at the Pyanj. Afghanistan remained a mystery to them. Like most Central Asians, they thought of Afghanistan as nothing more than a violent, lawless shithole where life is cheap and the principal export is heroin, and thus to be avoided by sane people. There is, of course, more to Afghanistan than that. Much more. The Central Asians shared a common border and heritage with Afghanistan, yet they pretended it didn't exist. They assumed I had a death wish. Why else would anyone go to such a terrible place populated by such violent people? Of course, they were at least partly right.

I resigned myself to playing things by ear. My old Tajik fixer, Sadoullo, would arrange for me to get from Dushanbe to the Afghan border. Then I'd be on my own. Afghans are industrious. I'd find people to drive and translate after I arrived "in country," as they say.

In the midst of my planning, I got a call from Steven Cloud. Cloudy, as his friends call him, was a brilliant cartoonist who drew a webcomic called *Boy on a Stick and Slither*. Cartooning is a small profession yet is balkanized into numerous genres and associated factions. Editorial cartoonists at daily newspapers all know or know of one another; they don't know many editorial cartoonists at the alternative weeklies. One rift is between cartoonists who work primarily in print media and the so-called webcartoonists, artists whose work appears exclusively online. I thought Cloudy, whose strip reminded me of the best *Peanuts* pieces from the 1960s, belonged in print. Quiet, effortlessly droll, and sporting a Nebuchadnezzar-worthy beard guaranteed to impress even in the hip Brooklyn neighborhood where he lived, he was hard to read but a straightforward and genuine guy.

In '09 Cloudy had taken his first major trip, for a charity. Participants in the Mongol Rally flew to Eastern Europe, bought a car, and drove it across Russia and Central Asia to Ulan Bator, capital of Mongolia. They were supposed to sell it in Ulan Bator. The trip had been predictably arduous but whetted his appetite for adventure in general and Central Asia in particular. When he heard I was taking Matt to Afghanistan, he wanted to come too. "Since I got back," he told me, "I haven't felt alive." I knew that feeling. I'm the same way whenever I don't have plans to leave for some new, interesting, and hopefully dangerous place.

I didn't know Cloudy well. He seemed nice enough, but we'd be going to a war zone. I hadn't seen him operate much at all, much less under stress. If the right traveling companion could save your life, the wrong one could get you killed. What if he was reckless? Or worse, a coward? Or worst of all, a whiner? What if he acted like the jerk on *Stan Trek 2000*, the one who thought he knew everything, because he'd driven across the Asian continent a year earlier? There was also the Rule of Three, the tendency of two to gang up against the third. It's the reason it's easier for roommates to live in pairs or multiples of two. Even if you're one of the two it isn't much fun to be a part of a trio.

Another concern was mobility and practicality. I knew from experience that sometimes you have to grab your stuff, throw it in a car, and get out of Dodge before the pitchfork-wielding (or AK-47-brandishing) townspeople come for you. Three people move exponentially slower than two. Sometimes you want to rent a small jeep and driver; the driver can fit two passengers and their gear, not three. Three guys means 50 percent more chance of someone doing something stupid or annoying or becoming a liability by, for example, falling ill or getting injured.

I had Cloudy out to my house for the weekend. We never talked about it but I knew that he knew that I was auditioning him for the trip. It was clear from his stories about the Mongol Rally that he knew how to be tough when a situation called for it—or at least to be quiet. Which is all one can ask. I also liked the way he thought. He had a highly adaptable personality, able to turn on a dime in response to changing conditions. And, like me, he was inclined to throw money at problems. Many Westerners, particularly Europeans, seem allergic to paying a few hundred bucks in bribes to get out of (or into) a sticky situation. They want to sleep for free even if it means risking their lives. Cloudy was old enough, and financially solvent enough, to pay to make good things happen (and avoid bad ones). I invited him along.

Why not? He had one hell of a beard.

THE GREAT DISRUPTOR
WHY THE UNITED STATES CAN'T TALK TO THE TALIBAN
JULY 1, 2010

Like all Afghans, Hamid Karzai knows history. Which is why he's talking to the neo-Taliban. The postmodern heirs to the Islamist government Bush deposed in 2001, the generation of madrassa graduates who replaced the mujahideen vets of the anti-Soviet jihad are gaining strength. Obama, preparing for his 2012 reelection campaign by distancing himself from an unpopular war, plans to start pulling out U.S. troops next year.

Men like Karzai, puppets of foreign occupiers, rarely die of old age in their beds, especially in Afghanistan. Mohammad Najibullah, the former Soviet-appointed head of the secret police who became president under the occupation, was extracted from a U.N. compound where he had taken refuge when Kabul fell in 1996. The Taliban dragged him from the back of a jeep, disemboweled him, cut off his penis, and forced him to eat it before hanging him from a lamppost.

Cutting a power-sharing deal with the Taliban may not be possible. But Karzai has to try.

His American overseers, though, are against dialogue. "With regards to reconciliation," CIA director Leon Panetta told ABC's *This Week*, "unless [the neo-Taliban is] convinced that the United States is going to win and that they're going to be defeated, I think it's very difficult to proceed with a reconciliation that's going to be meaningful."

We Americans have heard this line of policy so often that we don't think to question it. Never negotiate from a position of weakness. First thrash your adversary. Negotiate afterward.

Insisting upon "peace with honor," Nixon took Kissinger's advice to bomb the hell out of North Vietnam before the Paris peace talks. There's a certain logic to this approach, but no common sense. Three years later, the United States lost the same as if it had never dropped a single bomb.

John McCain echoed Nixon at a Senate hearing this week: "If the president would say that success in Afghanistan is our only withdrawal plan—whether we reach it before July 2011, or afterward—he would make the war more winnable and hasten the day when our troops can come home with honor, which is what we all want."

Win. Then withdraw.

Weird.

The best time to talk to your opponent—assuming that he's willing to take your calls—is when you're losing. Any concession you gain will be more than you'll otherwise end up with.

If you're going to win a war, on the other hand, why talk? When the United States is winning, it refuses to negotiate. Certain of victory, it insisted upon the unconditional surrender of Japan and Germany in 1945.

Panetta's statement provides two insights to those who seek to understand U.S. foreign policy.

On a basic level, it parrots Kissinger: The United States knows that it will lose in Afghanistan. Withdrawal is inevitable; indeed, it has been announced. America's next step is a massively violent final offensive—in order to prove to the neo-Taliban that it *could* win if it really wanted to. So they'd better cut us some slack: oil, gas, and mineral concessions, etc. Of course, this reflects a radical misreading of the neo-Taliban as well as of human nature. They understand the simple truth: they live there, and we don't. Time is on their side. The oppressor's greatest weakness is his inability to see things from a different point of view.

Moreover, bomb-first-then-talk is a (partly delusional) lie. If by some miracle the upcoming anti-Afghan offensive were to work, the United States would never open talks with the neo-Taliban. Whenever the United States thinks it holds the upper hand—Cuba since 1962, Iran since 1980, Iraq before the 2003 invasion—it refuses to engage. Only when something tips the balance in favor of a U.S. adversary—North Korea's development of nuclear weapons, for example—is it willing to chat.

More broadly and interestingly, the Panetta Doctrine helps us resolve the big mystery of U.S. actions abroad after 1945.

The United States hasn't won a war since World War II. More curiously, it doesn't seem to want to. When the United States invades, it often fails to occupy, much less annex. When it occupies, it does so with fewer soldiers than necessary to control its newly acquired territory. (Note that General Colin Powell, a rare proponent among the military elite of "flooding the zone" with hundreds of thousands of troops to ensure total domination of occupied countries, was quickly replaced as chairman of the joint chiefs of staff. His Powell Doctrine, though romanticized by some members of the press, is now forgotten.)

The United States has been described as an "empire without empire." It is more accurate to call it the Great Disrupter. It's fairly safe to conclude that United States' primary foreign policy objective is to disrupt potentially emerging regional rivals. Iran, for example, is the nation that should logically dominate the Middle East politically and economically. It possesses immense wealth, enviable geography, five thousand years of civilization, modern infrastructure, and a big, highly educated workforce. The United States uses sanctions to prevent Iran's rise to regional superpower.

You didn't really think we were still holding a grudge over those hostages, did you?

From a geopolitical standpoint, U.S. policymakers are far more concerned about India's potential role as the leader of South Asia than the threat that North Korea will nuke Seattle. Which is why the Bush administration sent billions of dollars in military hardware and cash subsidies to the violently anti-Indian government of General Pervez Musharraf after 9/11. Now Musharraf is out and the current Pakistani government has reduced its pressure on India via, for example, its support for Muslim fighters in Kashmir. So Obama continues to finance Pakistan—but not as much.

Naturally, we can't talk to the neo-Taliban. (Nor can we let Karzai do so.) An Afghanistan that resumes its 1996-to-2001 role as the global capital of Islamist government and Sharia law could represent a new kind of influence—simultaneously religious, political, and military—that the United States fears as much as Iran, India, or any other country big enough to suck away American market share.

I always plan ahead. But it never prevents crazy last-second scrambles. The weeks before my August 1 departure were filled with anxiety over two issues: Iranian visas and trying to find a venue to distribute my stuff from Afghanistan.

Our itinerary required us to leave Afghanistan via the western border with Iran. Officially speaking, there is no reason a U.S. citizen cannot visit Iran. Trade sanctions don't affect tourism, much less journalism, and Iran officially welcomes American visitors. Reality is different.

According to the Iranian government's website, Americans are required to mail in an application along with a fairly steep fee to the Iranian Interests section in the Pakistani embassy in Washington. A few weeks later my materials came back in the mail. Attached was a cryptic note: "Minors under 18 need parents' permission."

Rejected.

At twenty-seven, Matt Bors was the youngest of us three. I called repeatedly. During official hours. The phone would pick up. A recording would come on: "Thank you for calling the Iranian Interests section. Goodbye." Click. Disconnect.

I am not easily dissuaded. I was familiar with this fuck-off-and-die style of diplomacy from my dealings with the Kyrgyz embassy. I called and called and called and then, one day, amazingly, a guy picked up the phone. "Journalist?" he barked. "You apply to New York." So I called Iran's permanent mission to the U.N. in New York. And called. And called and called and called and, one day, amazingly, a different guy answered. "All visas go through Washington," he said, helpfully providing me with the D.C. number no one ever answers.

Weeks passed. Eventually I scored an appointment with a press attaché in New York. He was a gracious man, very nice and courteous and professional, and he promised to send my stuff to the staff in D.C., who would then get it approved by the Ministry of Foreign Affairs in Tehran (plus four of Iran's redundant intelligence agencies), who would then issue a magic number I could use to apply for an actual visa, which I'd have to travel to D.C. to pick up.

But less than a week before departure, there was still no word from the Iranians. I called my attaché. "Do not worry, my friend," he assured me. "You will have everything before you leave."

"But I leave Sunday. Which means I would need to go to Washington Friday. Which means I would need the number Thursday. Which is tomorrow."

Long pause. Then: "You really should have planned ahead." Five months wasn't planning ahead?

Steven saved the day. Days of research online revealed a sketchy Tehran-based tour agency that could get the visa approval numbers within a day or two, provided they were paid thousands of dollars for a tour of Iranian archeological sites. We paid.

My other concern was finding a home for the work I would file from Afghanistan. I wanted to post the cartoons somewhere with bigger distribution than my blog. I sent pitch letters to the approximately one hundred newspapers that ran my syndicated cartoons and columns, as well as to the other thirteen hundred that didn't. In all I got four replies. I don't know why. Was it because they were so broke they were reflexively saying no to everything, or because they didn't like my work, or because they didn't care about Afghanistan?

SO MUCH STUPIDITY

ON AFGHANISTAN, DEMOCRATS AND REPUBLICANS
    EQUALLY DUMB

JULY 7, 2010

As I pack for my return trip to Afghanistan next month, many people are asking me: Why are we losing? What should we do there?

The short answer is simple: Afghan resistance forces live there. We don't. Sooner or later, U.S. troops will depart. All the Afghan resistance has to do is wear us down and wait us out. As I have pointed out before, no nation has successfully invaded and occupied any other nation since the nineteenth century. All occupations ultimately fail.

For those who prefer their punditry long-winded, here's a longer answer:

Even taking historical precedent into account, America's post-9/11 occupation of Afghanistan—its longest war ever—has been notably disastrous. Wonder why? Everything you need to know was contained in this week's war of words between the chairmen of the two major political parties.

The Afghan War kerfuffle that revealed the boundless stupidity of our national political leadership began on July 1. Republican National Committee chairman Michael Steele told GOP donors in Connecticut that the war in Afghanistan could not be won and should never have been fought: "If [Obama is] such a student of history, has he not understood that, you know, that's the one thing you don't do is engage in a land war in Afghanistan? All right? Because everyone who's tried, over a thousand years of history, has failed," Steele said.

Steele's main point is beyond dispute. There's a reason Afghanistan is known as "the graveyard of empires," as opposed to, say, the "number one producer of tasty, nutritious pomegranates."

Steele's all too typical ahistoricity is in the details. Which he gets wrong.

Would-be conquerors have had trouble with Afghanistan not for one thousand years, but for two thousand years. Alexander the Great sent supplies through the Khyber Pass in 327 B.C.E. in an attempt to subjugate the Konar Valley. Characteristically, the locals waged a ferocious resistance. The Macedonian conqueror, nearly killed by an Afghan arrow, beat a retreat to the Indus River and withdrew.

But it's Steele's "land war" qualifier that really gets me. According to the GOP chairman, the British Army might have spared itself total annihilation in 1842 if it had conducted an air war instead. Using what—hot air balloons?

Then things got *really* weird.

"This was a war of Obama's choosing," Steele said.

Huh?

True, Obama made the Afghan war his own by sending in more troops. But Bush started this mess. Doesn't Steele remember that? Or—this thought is even more frightening—does he really think *we* forgot?

"This is not something the United States has actively prosecuted or wanted to engage in," he continued. This surely comes as welcome news to the tens of thousands of Afghans killed by tens of thousands of American bombs. Chin up. Imagine how many more would have died if the United States had "actively prosecuted" this fiasco!

Not to be outdone in the moronitude department, Democratic National Committee spokesman Brad Woodhouse retorted that "we are there because we were attacked by terrorists on 9/11."

Um . . . We were attacked by Saudis and Egyptians. Who were trained and funded by Pakistanis. None of the major figures linked to 9/11—including Osama bin Laden—were in Afghanistan on 9/11. (Bin Laden was in a Pakistani military hospital in Islamabad.) By 9/11, both Al Qaeda training camps in Afghanistan had been closed. Al Qaeda's operations were based entirely in Pakistan.

Afghanistan had nothing to do with 9/11.

Nothing.

None of the Afghans I interviewed in November and December of 2001 had even heard of 9/11. None had heard of Al Qaeda. Other journalists reported the same thing.

We attacked Afghanistan for fun. To disrupt Iran and India. To test weapons that would be used against Iraq. To test the resolve of the American antiwar movement. And to build an oil and gas pipe-line between Central and South Asia.

Not because of 9/11.

Woodhouse continued: "It's simply unconscionable that Michael Steele would undermine the morale of our troops when what they need is our support and encouragement. Michael Steele would do well to remember that we are not in Afghanistan by our own choos-ing, that we were attacked and that his words have consequences."

Dubya—is that you?

Can we even tell which party is which anymore?

No wonder we're losing. The parties have forgotten what they stand for—and they never learned the history of the countries they invade.

I was also still worried about money. Twenty-six thousand dollars is a nice chunk of cash by any definition, but for this kind of expedition it wasn't going to be enough. Salvation came from the *Los Angeles Times*, for whom I was drawing cartoons as a freelancer, and EurasiaNet, a George Soros–funded website dedicated to news and analysis of events in ex-Soviet Central Asia that was running my cartoons. Both put up some money and, even more important, promised to give my Afghanistan drawings prominent placement online and, in the case of the *Times*, on the editorial page of the print edition. The alternative weekly news-paper in Boston, *The Weekly Dig*, also agreed to run them on their website.

The last financial piece to fall into place was an "if you find any-thing good send it to us" cash advance from a newspaper in Scotland and another one in India. The Scottish paper wanted me to let them know if I saw any Scottish troops (I didn't, but they let me keep the money anyway). The Indian paper, which made me promise not to men-tion them because of their shady financial dealings, always had trouble getting good coverage from Afghanistan—the fact that the name of the Hindu Kush mountain range means "killer of Hindus" pretty much tells you everything you need to know—and asked me to send them anything of interest.

The Indians asked me to drop by Mumbai en route, where a helpful editor opened a safe in his office and simply handed me a sheaf of hundred-dollar bills without bothering to count them.

THE IDIOCRACY FACTOR
HOW U.S. IGNORANCE HELPED DOOM THE AFGHAN WAR
JULY 29, 2010

Americans' lack of knowledge about Afghanistan is virtually limitless. Which matters, because the United States is at war there. And which explains why the American military is losing its longest war.

During my 2001 trip, when I covered the Taliban defeat at the battle of Kunduz for *The Village Voice* and KFI radio, I met a British reporter who offered an amusing prescription for American military action. "If the average American cannot identify three cities in a country," he suggested, "the United States should not invade it."

Given that the average American doesn't know their state capital, much less three cities in, say, Canada, this would transform us into a pacifist society overnight.

More appalling than Joe and Jane Sixpack's ignorance about Afghanistan is the doltishness of the media. If print and broadcast journalists get the facts wrong, how can the public (or the military) be expected to do better? To cite one tiny example, U.S. newspapers routinely refer to the citizens of Afghanistan as "Afghanis." Afghanis are the national currency; the people are Afghans.

On a broader level, the Afghan war document trove published by WikiLeaks has prompted many to ask: Why didn't the media question the war against Afghanistan before now?

Mostly, U.S. state media didn't want to know anything that questioned the Bush-Obama administration's official line: 9/11 came out of Afghanistan, we have to prevent Al Qaeda from turning the country into a land of terrorist jungle gyms, and oh, yeah, we should do something about opium and burqas too.

People like Ahmed Rashid, the Pakistani journalist who wrote *Taliban*, tried repeatedly to get the world to pay attention to a different take. Pakistan, not Afghanistan, was the real danger in the region. In Afghanistan, the Karzai government was underfunded and overcorrupt and widely considered illegitimate. The United States sent in troops to shoot and bomb when they ought to have delivered construction equipment to build the infrastructure necessary to form a coherent state and a viable Afghan economy.

Rashid wrote books. Wonks bought them and read them. I wrote books. Ditto. But it didn't make a difference. It is shocking and disgusting that President Obama listened to people who know nothing about Afghanistan while ignoring those who do.

Countless personal experiences confirmed my impression that reporters "parachuted in" to cover wars for brief assignments could never deliver the nuanced, detailed, accurate coverage necessary for American leaders and the public to make informed decisions.

In 2001, CBS's correspondents sent to cover the invasion flew straight to Pakistan, only to get stuck there because the Khyber Pass was closed. (Anyone familiar with the region knew that.) I had a brief discussion with the network about my plan to go in via Tajikistan. A producer told me I would never make it. "The mountain passes are already snowed over," he said confidently, looking out his window at Manhattan traffic. "There's six feet of snow there." I made it. No snow. Not a single flake.

This reminds me of D-Day. Civil affairs detachments that accompanied the first wave of troops at Omaha Beach brought tons of food to feed French civilians, whom the Allied military believed to be starving. Though hunger was indeed widespread in occupied France, warehouses in Normandy were bursting with food; Allied bombing raids had cut the train lines that carried Norman produce to the rest of France. "Plenty of food," officers wired Eisenhower. "Send shoes."

French feet hadn't seen new shoes for four years.

I'm leaving for South Asia on August 1 and expect to be in Afghanistan for a month, beginning on or about August 13. Accompanied by fellow cartoonists Matt Bors and Steven L. Cloud, I'm going to take advantage of new satellite technology to upload a new kind of daily war correspondency to my blog (www.rall.com/rallblog) and a half dozen newspapers: a recounting of the day's events in comic form. I'll be going to the most remote parts of the country—the north and western villages and towns that see few if any visits by Western reporters. Why? Because they see few if any visits by Western reporters.

Pitching papers on this project has proven that little has changed since 2010: editors and producers are still clueless. Among some of the more priceless responses I've gotten:

"Do they take American Express there?" (No credit cards. Cash only.)

"How about if you call us and pitch us if you see something interesting?" (No phones.)

"Do you speak Pashto?" (No, but neither do Afghans in the north or west.)

"You'd be safer if you were embedded." (U.S. troops are the main target. Embedded reporters get hurt more often than independents.

And of course it's impossible to be objective, or speak freely with locals, when you're traveling with soldiers.)

But nothing speaks louder than the lack of interest in this project by the vast majority of media outlets. They'll keep talking about Afghanistan—but they won't put up the bucks to find out what's really going on.

TWO: RETURN OF THE WAR TOURIST

Travelers are under the ongoing threat of kidnapping and assassination in Afghanistan. Former Taliban and Al Qaeda operatives remain at large, and attacks with improvised explosive devices and vehicle-borne improvised explosive devices are increasing in frequency, according to the State Department. Areas most vulnerable to attack include domestic and international government centers, and the U.S. Embassy in Afghanistan frequently bans its employees from entering areas considered to be particularly risky.
— *Forbes*, February 16, 2006, explaining its selection of Afghanistan as the world's most dangerous travel destination

Before 2008, travelers to Tajikistan were forced to endure the horrors of Tajikistan Airlines, one of the "Baby Flots" that split off from Aeroflot at the time of the Soviet breakup. Tajik Air, as it is also known, offered the same ancient Tupolev 154s and hardboiled, chain-smoking "sky waitresses" as Aeroflot, minus the safety and elegance. The open kitchen galley was littered with half-eaten chicken bones. Most of the seats were broken and had no safety belts. On a flight from Moscow to Dushanbe in 2007, the rear windows were broken. We flew in depressurized minus-forty-degree frost for six hours. Then there was the time the pilot came back to talk to the passengers, so smashed he was visibly reeling, holding a plastic bottle of vodka.

I decided we'd try out the brand-new Somon Air, a timid competitor

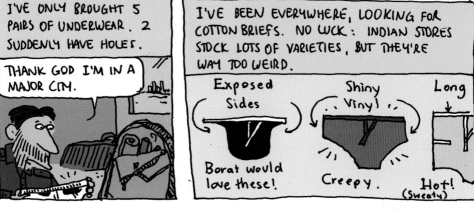

TAJIKISTAN MINUS A DAY: MATT IS SITTING ON AN AEROFLOT FLIGHT FROM PORTLAND TO NEW YORK TO MOSCOW TO DUBAI.

HE'S WITH STEVEN. I WORRY ABOUT MATT.

STEVEN IS A TROUPER. HE'S EXPERIENCED. THIS IS MATT'S FIRST FLIGHT OUTSIDE THE U.S. HE GOT HIS FIRST PASSPORT FOR THIS TRIP.

YOU'LL GIVE ME MY PASSPORT IN DUBAI, RIGHT?

NO, I'LL FEDEX IT. HOW WILL YOU GET ON THE FLIGHT?

WILL HE SUCCUMB TO THE TEMPTATION TO VEG OUT THE WHOLE WAY, THUS NOT DRINKING ENOUGH WATER, AND GETTING CLOBBERED BY JETLAG?

CAN...NOT...SLEEP.

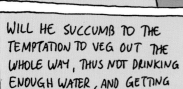

WILL HE FREAK OUT WHEN CONFRONTED BY HEAVILY ARMED, BRAZENLY CORRUPT AIRPORT COPS IN TAJIKISTAN? WILL HE GET THE DIARRHEA THAT WON'T QUIT?

Desperately clenching internal organs on bouncy Afghan truck →

MY INSTINCT TELLS ME THAT PERSONALITY IS DESTINY, THAT MATT IS MENTALLY CENTERED, AND YOUNG, AND WILL BE FINE.

привет!

AND YET...

10 EYE DOCTORS FOR A CHRISTIAN NGO HAVE BEEN SHOT BY THE NEO-TALIBAN IN NURISTAN. THAT'S IN THE "NORMALLY CALM NORTH."

FORTUNATELY, WE'RE NOT CHRISTIAN. NO ONE WILL ACCUSE US OF PROSELYTIZING.

RATIONALIZATION MAKES THE WORLD GO AROUND.

TAJIKISTANI PASSPORT CONTROL OFFICE, 100 M. NORTH OF THE "FRIENDSHIP BRIDGE" SEPARATING TAJIKISTAN AND AFGHANISTAN: MY FIRST SHAKEDOWN.

YOU HAVE PRESENT FOR ME? DOLLARS?

EMPTY POCKETS, PLEASE.

WHAT? ER... NÉ.

At least 100°F. Third time lugging heavy bags to an office.

AMAZING: A CORRUPT COP WHO TAKES "NO" FOR AN ANSWER.

YOU LIKE T-SHIRTS? I HAVE T-SHIRTS.

I ♥ N Y

NO, AND ACTING STUPID.

ACROSS THE BRIDGE: AFGHANISTAN.

CHAIN-LINK FENCE ROLLS MUST'VE FALLEN OFF A TRUCK HERE.

Pyanj River

AFGHAN CUSTOMS.

THERE ARE 2 POSSIBLE DRIVERS. WE BARGAIN. $50 TO TALOQAN. WE'RE OFF.

Afghanistan

I'VE PLANNED FOR THIS TRIP. I'VE RESEARCHED. BUT NOTHING COULD PREPARE ME FOR WHAT WE ENCOUNTER: ROADS.

PAVED ROADS.

Kondoz 58
Kabul 355

MAGNIFICENTLY PAVED ROADS.

to Tajik Air that ran from Dubai to Dushanbe. Whenever I get the opportunity not to spend time in Moscow, I seize it. Somon had that off-the-grid quality common to Tajik enterprises: its much-vaunted "online booking" didn't work for credit cards and the company wasn't listed in the directory of the Dubai airport. But the trip was grand, i.e., uneventful. After the terrible tales with which I had regaled Steven and Matt, travel on a perfectly clean, competently staffed, and reasonably modern airplane was anticlimactic.

It became a trend. Having warned my companions about the grim Soviet-style accommodations at the Hotel Tajikistan, where I'd stayed in 2001 and 2007, I booked us into the brand-new Hyatt Regency Dushanbe for two nights of five-star luxury before the hardships of Afghanistan. We were staring down the barrel of week after week of sleeping on dusty floors, eating crappy food, maybe not even being able to find enough water. Not to mention the constant threat of murder or kidnapping. I kept thinking about 2001, about how even a single night in Afghanistan seemed to take years off your life. I worried about Matt and Steven, especially since they were recovering from the kind of jet lag you can't possibly understand until you've traveled halfway around the planet.

Unlike the DWB doctors who were blowing through donor money, I wanted to make sure that the Kickstarter money got used as judiciously as possible. But I didn't want to lose my two traveling companions in the process. So I made the decision to spring for these nights of rest and relaxation before heading off on our grueling journey.

I've stayed in some nice hotels. The Hyatt Regency Dushanbe blew them all away.

Last breakfast at the Hyatt Regency Dushanbe, Tajikistan. We entered Afghanistan that afternoon.

Sumptuously and tastefully decorated in a boutique-hotel-cum-Eurasian-classic motif, frosted glass and earth tones everywhere, every detail from the light switches to the glasses at the bar *just so*, with heated floors and walk-in closets and wifi and a world-class spa, a thirty-seven-inch flat screen television hanging from the wall of every room, I asked myself: What the hell is this place doing here? Tajikistan's average salary of six hundred dollars a month is ranked one hundred ninetieth in the world. The country has no significant natural resources to speak of, certainly no oil or gas. Why would the Hyatt chain invest millions of dollars on a hotel so certain to remain mostly empty?

The answer, I learned (or, more precisely, I was told by enough well-placed locals to judge the story credible), was that this was President Emomali Rahmon's latest vanity project. Such are the benefits of authoritarian rule. Dushanbe neither needs nor can justify a five-star hotel with rooms going for four hundred bucks plus a night. But Rahmon wanted one. So he bought one. They bought a license to use the Hyatt name, hired an upscale architecture firm from Ohio to design something jazzy, and threw millions of *somoni* at it. So what if there weren't enough *biznezmen* in all of Central Asia, much less Tajikistan, to make it fiscally viable? It existed. That was enough. "In a few years," a typically cynical NGO exec stationed in Dushanbe told me over twenty-four-dollar glasses of chardonnay (her treat, not mine) by the charcoal pit in the outdoor plaza bar, "this place will be falling apart. That's how it always goes. We know it. They know it. So it goes on and on and on."

The breakfast buffet was divine. The apples were not merely organic, they were *real*—small and juicy and imperfect and local. A chef stood at the ready to create omelets, French toast, waffles, anything. The coffee was strong but not bitter, sweet but sturdy. Matt, Steven, and I marveled, taking photos of the food, amazed at the incongruity with the grinding poverty in the city outside, every bit the condemned men eating a final, ridiculously delicious meal. Across the marble floor was a long table with the only other diners, a dozen American soldiers. They were stationed at a nearby French-NATO airbase.

"Check out the heroes," Matt snarked. "Standing tall, defending America's freedoms on the front lines of the war on terror." We looked around. Could the chef be a Talib? He didn't *look* like a Talib.

"It's kind of crazy," said Steven. "We're paying four hundred a night for these guys?"

"We?" I laughed. "Who's we?" I wasn't paying taxes. I had been laid off from my day job as a comics editor/talent scout a year earlier.

Sadoullo was tied up in Tashkent, so he arranged for a friend to drive us to the Afghan border. The requirement for special permits to cross the demarcation line a hundred kilometers away from Afghanistan was history; now you get in the car, your driver bribes the cops at checkpoints, very straightforward. Unlike 2001, when the road turned to

New NATO-built road from the Tajik-Afghan border to Taloqan

mud and rocks just outside Dushanbe, it's mostly paved now. The old tractor barge across the Pyanj has been replaced by a new Tajik-Afghan Friendship Bridge built by the Aga Khan, Norway, and the United States to the east. The Russians—er, Soviets—have gone home.

The Tajik *militsia* (military police) guard the border. Which means that the crossing has become just like any other frontier in former Soviet Central Asia: ratty, full of redundant checkpoints, each staffed by bored, drunk, corrupt cops whose primary duty is to intimidate travelers into coughing up "gifts" before they're permitted to continue on their

own. Between the weather (around a hundred degrees in the theoretical shade), lugging boxes of bottled water and other gear, and the stress of the shakedowns, sweat was pouring off us when we arrived at the Darvaz customs house. Surprisingly—though nominally secular, Tajikistan has a conservative streak, especially outside the capital—there were both a man and a woman working there.

"Where are you leaving Afghanistan? Kabul?" the male Afghan asked me.

"Iran."

Goodbye, Hyatt.

He broke into a wide, typically Afghan, sarcastic smile. "But you are American."

"*Ho,*" I affirmed in Dari.

"You have visa for Iran?"

"*Ho.*" I handed him our passports to the relevant page.

Surprised laughter. "How did you get Iranian visas? Americans can*not* get them. I am here since Taliban time. Never an American can go to Iran."

"We are special." I winked.

Afghans are brutal negotiators. There was only one taxi in the parking lot. So the driver knew we needed him. On the other hand, we were the only foreigners. He needed us, too. Anywhere else, this balance would result in a fair price for the trip we requested, back to Taloqan. (My plan was to find my 2001 fixer, Jovid, and hire him or someone close to him for the remainder of our journey.)

Either Afghans aren't like anyone else or they're amazing bluffers.

Site of the 2001 battle of Khanabad as seen in 2010

They would rather starve (or that's the way they play it) than take less than what they want for a good or a service—a rate that is almost invariably outrageously high. This is particularly true when dealing with foreigners, whom they view as human ATMs. Time after time, I've seen them walk away from paydays most Americans would be thrilled to take.

I don't understand it. I know what it's like to be poor and desperate. Hell, I know what it's like to be *upper middle class* and desperate. When I need cash, I don't negotiate hard. I want the work no matter what—well, unless the rate is so ridiculously low that it would be insulting or would waste time I could spend finding something better. But Afghans don't roll that way. By some accounts their national unemployment rate is one hundred percent. Yet they make no serious attempt to negotiate.

Culturally and geographically, Afghanistan is split. The north is properly part of Central Asia. It has the same steppes and grasslands and even some of the natural gas and oil reserves found in the Caspian Sea basin. The population is largely composed of Central Asian tribesmen: Tajiks, Uzbeks, Turkmen. The nation south of the Hindu Kush, on the other hand, is South Asian, having more in common with Pakistan. It is hot and dusty and primarily Pashtun. Ever since the Brits drew the Durand Line separating Afghanistan from northwestern India (now Pakistan) in 1893, Pashtuns have dreamed of reuniting the land they call Pashtunistan.

Kunduz province, where we entered from Tajikistan, is dominated by the Tajiks. Ahmed Shah Massoud, the Northern Alliance warlord assassinated two days before the 9/11 attacks and now a sort of patron saint of the Karzai government, was Tajik.

In Tajikistan a taxi ride equivalent to the one we wanted to Taloqan should cost a foreigner about ten or fifteen bucks. Not in Afghanistan.

"You pay me one hundred dollars each," the driver insisted. A small crowd gathered around as we talked. "Yes! You are Americans. Americans are rich," a young man added.

"Twenty dollars for all of us," I said.

"Okay," he said, "but fifty dollars for each of your bags." We each had three. I laughed, trying to appear authentically relaxed. In reality, I was nervous about the time. You never want to be outside at night in Afghanistan. I figured Taloqan to be a couple of days away over the same set of backbreaking roads I remembered from 2001. It was already about two. That left three hours at most to find a place to sleep. I didn't want to lose this guy; spending the night at the customs hall wouldn't be much fun—or smart.

When I began planning the trip I picked Kunduz and Takhar provinces as our entry point because they were relatively calm. By August 2010, however, the situation had changed. On July 2, a Taliban suicide assault team attacked a company working for USAID, killing an Afghan soldier, a policeman, and two company contractors. On July 24, Talibs overran a police checkpoint in Baghlan province, just next door, and beheaded six cops. On August 5, a suicide bomber rammed his car into a police convoy, killing seven more cops in Imam Sahib district. Imam Sahib was one of the five districts in the province considered under complete Taliban control. Kunduz has seven districts.

One week later, the Taliban made international headlines by publicly stoning to death a young couple who had eloped in a village in northern Kunduz. The action was notable for its brazenness—it was carried out in broad daylight before hundreds of villagers—and the evident approval of the local population. According to reports, about two hundred people, including members of the pair's family, participated. "We see it as a sign of a new confidence on the part of the Taliban in the application of their rules, like they did in the '90s," Nader Nadery, senior commissioner with the Afghanistan Independent Human Rights Commission, told *The New York Times*. "They're showing more strength in recent months, not just in attacks, but including their own way of implementing laws, arbitrary and extrajudicial killings."

Another hour of negotiation followed. We settled on fifty, which I considered an act of extortion, and headed off toward Taloqan.

Why? I wondered.

Why hadn't the United States bragged more about the infrastructure it had built in Afghanistan?

Hundreds of miles of new roads where there had only been dirt tracks. Actual road signs and mile markers. New bridges everywhere. High-tension pylons parallel to the highway announced an electrified future, although there weren't any wires yet. The difference was startling. The donkeys were gone. So were most of the old Soviet cars and trucks. Modern cars and trucks plied the highways. Insofar as the

The many poses of candidates in Afghan political posters, from dapper to dour, businesslike to matinee idol. Note that liberal women candidates wear makeup and show hair.

roads went, Afghanistan had jumped from the Middle Ages straight into the twenty-first century. Early industrialization? No need.

There were shortcomings.

Evidence that civility had a long way to go included distance signs pasted over with posters for an upcoming parliamentary election. Afghan government gun nests every few kilometers testified to the risks associated with traveling these highways, but not nearly as much as the recently burned hulks of trucks, mostly oil tankers blown up by IEDs, lining the road.

In some areas the roadbed had been poorly laid, causing the asphalt to warp and roll as heavy vehicles passed over it. Through American eyes, the roads looked like they'd been done on the cheap. When I looked into it, this turned out to have been the case. In road construction the gold standard is poured concrete. It costs three times more than asphalt but it's durable and saves considerable money on maintenance. Afghanistan's new asphalt roads are cheap even by their own standards, just one layer. The harsh climate and use of the "ring road" highways between major cities by tanks and other heavy military vehicles are accelerating the wear and tear. According to USAID, maintaining America's gift roads will cost the Afghan government $1 billion every five years. In a country with an annual federal budget of $7 billion, this is a terrible burden.

Still, the fact that the roads were shoddy shouldn't distract too much from the fact that they were there at all. In 2001 all you heard was Afghans—and everyone else—complain about the state of the roads, or the lack thereof. Distances that used to take days to travel could now be covered in an hour or two. It was a remarkable cultural transformation, allowing people who had never left their province to travel hundreds of miles away. It is impossible to overstate the magnitude of this achievement or its implications.

Most of the Afghans I talked to about the road didn't know about

Broken down near Khanabad, shattered by battle in 2001, now lush

this. In any case, they were surprisingly unimpressed. In '01 all anyone talked about was roads, roads, roads. Give us roads, people told me over and over, and we will be able to revive trade. The country will be connected. Warlordism, which partially relies on cutting a nation into disconnected fiefdoms, would end as a result.

Reactions to the new roads were about evenly divided between Afghans who thought they were too little, too late and those who thought the roads actually hurt them. The latter argument was articulated by a piece in the *Kabul Press*, which asserted that paving the ring road "will spur imports of luxury goods that benefit the rich; it will suck financial capital out of the country; it will provide the Taliban with a constant flow of revenue, and it is already being used by criminal organizations, who can move goods and people more freely throughout the country." The broader subtext, I think, is that Afghans were disgusted by a government and an occupation that empowered the brutish new upper classes at their expense while failing to take even token measures to help the one-third of the population that suffered from hunger every day. "What good are roads?" the owner of a small store selling jackets asked me. "Only the rich can afford a car." But roads were an improvement, even if you could only afford to ride the bus. His colleague chimed in. "It is not all bad," he said. "Sometimes the Taliban use the roads to kill the rich people in their cars."

War is not as disruptive to everyday life as you might assume. Especially conflicts between insurgents/guerrillas/freedom fighters/whatever and conventional armed forces. Unlike a traditional battlefield, as in 2001, on which adversaries face one another and fire projectiles back and forth, life looks normal. Shops are open, streets are jammed with cars, guys argue and laugh on the streets about whatever. Most of the time, nothing happens. Until it does: usually a random explosion or sudden burst of gunfire somewhere nearby, ideally not too close. Insurgent warfare feels less like war than life in the worst neighborhood you could possibly imagine. There's lots of crime, mostly murder and attempted murder, not so much robbery.

What's the difference between Taloqan and the Central Parkway neighborhood of Cincinnati, where residents faced a one-in-four chance of becoming the victim of a violent crime in 2011? Tension.

Cincinnatians take grim (and somewhat unrealistic) comfort in their ability to avoid trouble. They stay in at night. They avoid drugs and those who deal in them. They eschew gang colors. The odds are bad, but they can take action to improve them. The residents of Taloqan in August 2010, on the other hand, knew that their destinies were not their own. You can't help going to the bazaar; that's where food is. Every now and then, however, some asshole sets off a bomb or opens fire there. No one knows why. You can't stay home all the time; life in Afghanistan requires taking to the roads to visit relatives or conduct commerce. That checkpoint ahead? Could be members of the

Taloqan, controlled by the Northern Alliance in 2001, by the Taliban in 2010

neo-Taliban, a frightening blend of Islamist fanaticism and opportunist thuggery. They might wave you by, or they might pull you out of your vehicle, rape your wife while you're forced to watch, then execute you. Or they might be Afghan national policemen. Will they be satisfied with a modest gratuity, or will they rob you of your life savings? Anything is possible.

Taloqan's nickname in 2001 was "town of donkeys." The scruffy beasts were everywhere. Kids and old men rode them. They pulled carts. Bigger ones were groomed and decked out with red pom-poms. They plied the muddy ruts they called roads past the ruins of one-story buildings pockmarked by automatic weapons fire. By the time Matt, Steven, and I rolled into town nine years later, Taloqan had exploded into a bustling sprawl of cars, motorcycles, and motorized rickshaws imported from Pakistan. All the main roads, and many side streets, had been paved. Electrical wires snaked from storefront to storefront. There were more stores than I could count. The Taliban would not be pleased at what was on offer: music and video CDs, machines to play

Note the Internet ad.

Afghan traffic cop, Taloqan

Televisions were banned by the Taliban, yet are sold openly during the day.

them on, television sets. Cellphone towers sprouted like dandelions across every mound of dirt; signal strength registered at four bars more consistently than in Los Angeles.

According to official sources, Taloqan was under government control. At first glance, it looked that way. Election posters hung from wires over the streets. Government cops manned the major traffic circles. Men stared at us as we passed, but so what? Taloqan is fairly remote. They don't see many foreigners.

The Taliban belied the oft-stated claim that democracy is the mid-wife of capitalism. Bazaars and shops bustled during the day. At night, however, many of those government policemen *became* the Taliban. They dragged women they called wanton and men judged to be unreli-able into the night, some never to be seen again, others to turn up later, missing body parts more often than not.

The Taliban had quite cannily created a shadow government across the country, ready to step into power the moment Karzai and his fel-low puppets fled into exile or met their comeuppance, complete with business cards and custom letterhead; a shadow (Taliban) deputy min-ister of communications for Takhar province had issued an edict ban-ning cellphone service at night. The telecom providers, headquartered in faraway Delhi and Zurich, complied. The official minister of com-munications for Takhar remained prudently silent.

Everyone was terrified. Women all wore burqas. It was as if the Taliban had never left in 2001. Which, in more than one sense, they never had. In 2001 there still remained a healthy fear of the Taliban. But most people here were hopeful, and happy to see their influence wane under the pressure of American bombs. Predominantly Takhar had chafed under the rule of the Pashtun-dominated Talibs from the south.

On that trip eight years earlier, over dinner at the home of my translator, Jovid, he had invited me to examine the family Koran. The holy book rested open on a stand. Under the stand was a box draped

Market, Taloqan

Afghans consume indigenous music, as well as pop from Indian and Pakistani films.

Despite U.S. news accounts, most women still wear the burqa, especially outside Kabul.

with an embroidered cloth. "Do you like our Koran?" Jovid asked. He lifted the stand and removed the drapery to reveal a small black-and-white television. Everybody laughed. "That's how we kept it throughout the Taliban period," he said.

There was no electricity. Nor was there a single channel on the air. The point wasn't to watch TV, but to retain the self-respect rooted in an act of rebellion. You can occupy our hometown. You can change our behavior. We may cringe when you pass. But you can't change who we are.

The Taliban, of course, were still around when Jovid showed me his Koran. They had been in charge days earlier. Many of them still lived there; when the Kandaharis withdrew, Taloqan's Talibs went home, shaved their beards, replaced their black turbans in favor of the rolled-up brown *pakul* hat popularized by Shah Massoud, and resumed their civilian lives. For that matter, most Northern Alliance troops were Talibs whose commanders had defected in exchange for cash, arms, and cars. It was a fluid mishmash of loyalties and opportunism; only those whose faces and darker skins marked them as foreign (the "Arabs," which in Afghan jargon included not only Saudis but Pakistanis, Uzbeks, Uyghurs, and Chechens) found it necessary to flee.

Though unpopular, especially in the north, Taliban strictures governing personal dress and religious behavior were rooted in the conventions of the dominant Pashtun culture, much of which has been adopted by other major tribes. In the same way that urbane young hipsters in American cities might roll their eyes at the conservative cornballery signified by flag-draped bunting and the endless ranting of Fox News "family values" barkers yet remain silent when their grandparents regurgitate Rush Limbaugh at family dinners, liberal Afghans sneak their hash and wine and porn DVDs rather than risk offending their conservative countrymen. Fear of the Taliban was coupled with tolerance for their intolerance. Gingerly modernization, rather than outright defiance, was the order of the day.

By 2010, however, growing, bustling, auto-choked Taloqan—almost unrecognizable—was a city on the brink of social collapse. Brazen Taliban attacks, focused mainly on Afghan police, NATO convoys, and fuel trucks, along with the obvious impotence and corruption of the only force that might have opposed them—the mostly absent central government—convinced anyone who was paying attention (in Afghanistan, attentiveness makes the difference between life and death) that Taloqan was close to succumbing to complete Taliban control.

People were so terrified that the town, which had served as the main headquarters for the entire international press corps covering northern Afghanistan in 2001 (which ended with them fleeing in panicked terror, with colleagues in coffins), didn't offer a single house or hotel willing to house a foreigner.

"You are foreigners?" a government traffic cop asked us, his widening eyes revealing his incredulousness as well as the hazard we were facing. "Foreigners do not come here. They cannot stay in the city of Taloqan."

For a brief moment it looked as though Afghanistan's long tradition of providing warm hospitality to beleaguered travelers was nonetheless going to land us a place to sleep. "My brother lives here," our driver told us. "You can stay with him."

We wove down a narrow side street, half cobblestones, half giant muddy holes covered with thin metal plates for cars such as ours, where no reconstruction funds had been spent. Our driver's brother's place was on the right at the end of a dead end. Kids played in the rapids of a small rushing stream perpendicular to the road.

The usual Afghan meet-and-greet ensued: leave your shoes at the door, find a spot leaning on a carpet pillow against the wall of a room containing nothing else but a red and black carpet. Check the soles of your feet; facing them toward a person is an insult. Watery tea all around. It's Ramadan (why the hell do I always wind up in Afghanistan during Ramadan?), so refuse, but your host insists you drink, you

In Afghanistan, even abstract symbols are skinny.

infidel you, and you're crazy thirsty so you do. Though you shouldn't. Invariably second and third waves of curious neighbors and random relatives file in. More introductions.

We were made to understand that this second-floor apartment—designed in Afghanistan's standard unfinished poured-concrete-floors-and-cracked-windows motif—doubled as the campaign headquarters of a second-tier actor who was living in exile (either in Spain or India, they couldn't get their story straight) and hoped to be elected as one of the city's representatives to the parliament in Kabul. "Please," implored the actor's nephew, whom we dubbed the Afghan doppelganger of Derrick Jensen, the environmentalist writer. "You must stay here with me."

Shortly after we arrived, however, cellphones began buzzing. Conversations in Dari, increasingly heated, ensued. No one would tell us what was going on. Finally, after another chat, our host gave us a sad puppy-dog face. "That was the city commander," he said, using the interchangeable term for a government official or district warlord. "The Taliban saw you coming," he said. "I am very sorry, and I am ashamed"—he paused for emphasis—"but the commander, he says if you are here tonight there will be trouble for all of us." He waved his hands around to encompass the neighbors and family members, all of whom had now exchanged their grins for somber you-had-so-better-get-the-fuck-out-of-here expressions.

Dark was an hour away. Kunduz, the nearest major city, was at least two hours west and was in any event even more Talibanized than Taloqan. The government didn't even bother to put on a good show at the traffic circle during the day. Calls were made. A gaudy wedding hall south of town agreed to put us up for a hundred bucks a night provided we agreed to maintain a low profile and avoid contact with American or NATO troops. "They have good security," assured our erstwhile host, now off the hook. The security turned out to be a skinny guy sitting on an office chair across the street from the gated entrance, brandishing an AK-47. "If the Taliban bring it," Steven observed, "I don't think that guy will be able or inclined to go down fighting."

In 2001 I stayed with a pharmacist in the center of town, across the street from the Red Crescent. The accommodations were primitive, but we'd gotten to meet ordinary people, watched them live their daily lives. To me, that's what made foreign travel worthwhile: the chance to get a brief glimpse of how people in other countries get by from day to day.

This experience, so valuable, was denied to us.

In 2010, Afghans were strictly prohibited from receiving foreigners as overnight guests. Only one hotel, the gaudy Ariana Hotel and Wedding Banquet Hall, would accommodate non-Afghans. "The situation in Taloqan is not good," continued the campaign manager. "At night."

We had the Ariana entirely to ourselves. Compared to the spartan conditions I endured nine years ago—bed lice, outhouse guarded by a mean rooster—it was a palace. Air-conditioning, real beds, no parasitic biters as far as I could tell. There was a generator to supplement the four hours a day of electricity supplied to the city. Everyone acted casual. Yet tension hung in the air. "Keep the curtains down," a young man told us. We knew why. "Don't leave your room." We got that too. Kebabs, soda, and nan bread arrived a little later. Room service!

It was a gilded cage, one surrounded by high walls topped with barbed wire and guarded by a caffeinated man brandishing an AK-47. We couldn't go out at night, and most Afghans didn't either. There was more prosperity. But it was even less safe.

You might get shot, even tortured first, but if you had the money, you could live decently before it happened.

THREE: JOVID, LOST

We know Ajmal's fate before the movie begins. He will be kidnapped. He will be held for ransom. He will be beheaded.
—From an online review of *Fixer: The Taking of Ajmal Naqshbandi* (2009)

My Last Day in Afghanistan, 2001

"They killed the Swede." Carmen, the sassy Moscow correspondent for a Portuguese radio network, let those words out in a rush as she appeared at my door. We collected details, such as they were: In the middle of the night, there'd been a knock at the door of the outer compound where Ulf Strömberg was staying. It was two doors down the street from our rented room. He answered. Two teenaged men, probably Northern Alliance soldiers, burst in. He ran to his house and slammed the door. The killers shot him through the door, stripped his body of cash and a sat phone, and fled.

We reporters congregated at the Ministry of Foreign Affairs, a grand title for the new government's administrative outpost, a second-floor office on an unnamed street outfitted with furniture that would have fitted in at one of Saddam's palaces, a bordello, or a crack house, depending on condition.

I was shaken. The Swede had died around 3:30 a.m. Someone had knocked at my outer door around three. I hadn't answered. I wasn't expecting anyone and it wasn't my house so it wasn't my place to open the door. "Say, Carmen," I asked, "did you get a knock at your door last night?" She had.

I polled the thirty or so journalists milling about. With the exception of the two big networks on the scene, ABC and the BBC—both were safely if unethically ensconced at the luxurious, complete with running water and flushing toilets compound of the local warlord—all had been awakened the previous night by the insistent knocks of two or three men at the walls of their compounds. Only Ulf had answered.

"My god," a writer for the British newspaper *The Guardian* said. "They know where all of us live."

"Tonight," added Carmen, "they will come for all of us. They will bring their friends."

"Unless we leave today," someone else said, "tonight's sunset will be the last one we see."

Word went around: we would form a convoy. We would hightail it back to the Tajik border. We'd have to be out of Afghanistan before dark.

I never understood, and still don't, war reporters' practice of traveling in long convoys of vehicles. If it seems as though there is safety in numbers, I don't see how. Big groups attract much more attention than individual cars and trucks.

It's not like it reduces the chances of you, as an individual, getting shot. Entire convoys have been wiped out. It happened in Cambodia in 1993. I might understand it if there were a mutual defense pact, preferably involving weapons. But that isn't the case. Prudent reporters covering Afghanistan, aware of Pashtunwali's dictum that the un-armed traveler is entitled to hospitality, do not carry firearms. Besides, if there is an attack on one vehicle, standard procedure is to abandon the doomed car and its occupants to their fates and speed off. But hey, groups just aren't my style.

"Fuck the convoy," I told my wife and agent, who had accompanied me against everybody's better judgment. I was starting to feel scared. And guilty. I turned to my fixer, Jovid. "Get me the shittiest-looking Soviet pickup truck you can find," I ordered, "and the ugliest, poorest driver. Tell him to invite anyone he wants to come along—men, women, and children—to the Tajik border. It's a free ride." Most of my colleagues, I knew, would go high profile: fancy SUVs with tinted windows, armored trucks with famous logos. Discretion only goes so far—if you're stopped at a checkpoint, whoever is manning it will soon learn the truth about your identity. As long as you keep moving, however, you buy a few precious seconds of doubt—"what th—?"—as you pass by people on the road.

We ran back to our room to change into local clothes. My wife, Judy, and my agent, Mary Anne, would ride in the front with the driver, wrapped up from head to toe. I'd ride in the back with the locals, covered in a *pakul* and wrapped in the traditional brown, green-fringed scarf of Takhar. We would remain silent even if spoken to.

Jovid reappeared thirty minutes later, driver and truck in tow. "Let's go," I said, banging the side of the truck. "We're not waiting for any stupid convoy."

I hunkered down. A couple of happy Afghan families, enjoying the free ride, tried to chat me up. *Quiet,* I motioned them. Finger to lips, then a slicing motion across my throat. I pointed at them. *If anyone finds out who I am, they'll kill you too.* Just outside town we encountered a checkpoint. Northern Alliance soldiers, obviously bored—not in the preferable way, in which they're too lazy to cause us trouble, but in the bad, scanning the horizon for something interesting to do, way. The driver turned around, speaking in Dari, smiling. Jovid translated: "I'll say you're idiots, can't talk, traumatized. Let me do the talking."

We slowed down, not stopping, and the driver yelled something at the soldier who came to talk to him. Then he floored the gas. Such as he could; we're talking maybe fifteen miles an hour. The driver smiled at me. "He told the soldier he couldn't stop the truck because then he couldn't start it again," Jovid informed me.

Slowly, steadily, we left the soldiers behind. We saw them cluster, discuss, point at us, discuss some more. Then they fired at us. We were maybe a soccer field away by this point, too far to catch on foot or to hit with bullets, but I heard them whiz by.

It was a long trip back to the border, hot and dusty, though not as terrible as three weeks earlier since the BBC truck wasn't there to kick up even more glacial flour. The sun arced across the robin's-egg sky of Central Asia, racing off to Iran as we banged our way back to the Pyanj. We made it back across the river without stalling.

We were making great time. We would have reached Tajikistan before sunset. Then, three kilometers from the border, we got lost. At this point I began to second-guess myself. Maybe the BBC had hired drivers who could find the border.

Dusk. We drove, circling along roads that separated freshly cultivated fields. No one was around. We were desperate. Then we saw the traffic cop.

He was the first uniformed official we had laid eyes upon since we had entered Afghanistan three weeks earlier. He was a glorious specimen, too: fat, decked out in a dark blue uniform resplendent with epaulets and giant medals, with a huge hat with some sort of shield on it, like a character from a Terry Gilliam film. He sat on a chair at the intersection of two dirt roads in the middle of nowhere, officious and incongruous.

I blinked. Was he real? He was.

We stopped to ask directions. The nineteenth-century cop stood up and pointed to the left.

"Ask him if he's sure," I told Jovid.

Our constable reconsidered. His arm waved around. Right, maybe. Or was it the way we'd come from?

Five painful minutes passed like this. Darker, darker, always darker.

Finally the driver pulled a large pistol out of his waistband and held it against the cop's chest. The cop, understandably, was not happy. He resisted. Jovid and the driver roughly shoved him into the front of the cab. Great. We'd kidnapped the only police officer in Afghanistan. Not that he had anything better to do.

Sussing out that I was in charge of his predicament, the policeman made imploring noises and gestures. "Tell him," I said to Jovid, "that if he does not give us directions to the border, we will kill him." I know. This is shocking to read. But you have to understand that this was fairly standard behavior. Whether crossed or disrespected or simply persuading an Afghan to do your bidding, a typical threat to kill them, their family, and everyone they'd ever met is usually issued. "But if he helps," I added, "we will pay him two hundred dollars." Which was more than he would have earned in two years as a civil servant, assuming he was paid.

A look of great concentration, new to him insofar as our experience was concerned, crossed the natty policeman's face. He'd been fucking with us.

We were at the border ten minutes later. I paid the cop. "Take him back where you found him," I told the driver. I gave Jovid a wad of hundreds to thank him for his service. We stood there.

"Ordinarily," I told Jovid, "in my country, we would exchange telephone numbers so we could see each other in the future. But there are no phones. Or you would give me an address. I would mail you a letter."

"We have no mail." Jovid smiled.

"Maybe there will be mail with the new government?"

"Maybe," he said.

"But you don't have an address," I said. "Your streets don't have names or numbers."

"No."

"Then this is it. Goodbye." We hugged. We embraced in the charming Tajik custom, one kiss on each cheek while holding hands.

He smelled awful. He *always* smelled bad. Early in our journey, Mary Anne and Judy, revolted by Jovid's b.o., had wanted to fire him. I resisted on the grounds of honesty: he was the only Afghan we'd met who'd never lied to us.

I couldn't say that about many Americans.

Also, I worried about Jovid. He was slight, and feminine, more fem even than the average Afghan guy. They can be pretty girly, even the tough ones. His father, he told me, didn't approve of his career plans. Rather than join a militia, which would provide a career as a robber, rapist, and murderer before leaving him dead under a pile of rocks someday, he studied English in the hope of becoming a professional translator.

Later, while we rode a donkey cart down a street, he pointed out a storefront: "My father's tailor shop." We went inside. His father had a long beard, like the guys in ZZ Top, and looked to be about eighty, which meant he was probably about fifty. "Your son is doing a very good job for me," I kind of lied to Jovid's dad. His English was objectively terrible. But you don't hire a fixer for his linguistic abilities. It's about contacts: Hey, I'd like to go to Mazar. No problem, my uncle lives there, we can stay with him. And if he's honest—and Jovid was—well, that's amazing. I added: "Jovid is good at the front."

"Good at the front" meant brave. At the front of the battle zone, some Afghans and many reporters would flinch and yell and generally panic whenever a shot rang out. If you were good at the front, it meant you were afraid—everyone was afraid—but you kept it to yourself. Everyone appreciated that.

"My father says it is okay for me to study English," he told me a few days later.

Taloqan, August 2010

Finding Jovid was one of three reasons I wanted to come back to Afghanistan. I wanted to make sure he was safe, to bring him money just to help out, to hire him as our fixer if he was available . . . and if he wasn't, to hire one of his friends.

My first stop was his father's tailor shop. The street grid was the same, but finding things was disorienting. The soccer field that had served as an execution site before '01 and as a helicopter landing pad during '01 was now an actual soccer field with green grass and bleachers and decorative shrubs. The Red Crescent hospital was still there, hidden behind a row of new buildings with copper-tinted mirrored glass windows. Now there were cars, so many cars, and rickshaws, and lots of honking. The Shah Massoud Restaurant, until recently the Mullah Omar, was gone, replaced by a row of stalls selling *shalwar kameez*es and the Chinese-made camouflage jackets, pants, and vests popular among men of a certain age (under thirty). I spun around. I talked to several shopkeepers. They all told me the same thing: the tailors were all gone.

"Ah, yes, I remember these tailor shops," a man told me. "Now they are jewelry stores."

School, Kabul

"Where did the tailor shops go?"

"Nowhere. A friend of a big commander, he owns these jewelry stores. He hired soldiers to get rid of the tailors. Those guys . . . not all of them are still alive."

I set out to find Jovid's house. I remembered it from 2001 because his family members had had to spirit us back across town to our guesthouse through two attempted ambushes. You never forget the first time someone shoots at you. Not a stray bullet. *Someone trying to kill you.*

Only a few piles of stones remained. "What happened to this house?" I asked a wary man who lived next door. Fire, he said. Another guy said it was a bomb. A third blamed an earthquake. Everyone

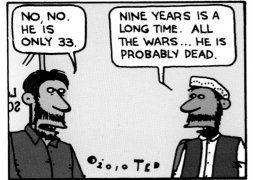

remembered Jovid's family, but no one could or would tell me what had become of them.

I wound up at Taloqan's sole remaining English language school. "He was a translator," my driver said. "If anyone in Taloqan knows anything about him, they will."

A bunch of English-language tutors filed into the room. I explained. They asked around. One guy said he thought he knew him. Everyone laughed when I said I didn't know Jovid's last name. Many Afghans use just one name, but Jovid is a very common name. "The Jovid I know," said the man in question, "he went to Kabul. He could not wait

Village destroyed by U.S. carpet bombing in 2001, Kunduz province

to leave Taloqan." Sounded like my Jovid. He gave me a mobile phone number. I called. There was no answer.

The head tutor looked at me. "I think your Jovid is dead," he said. A sad smile. "This is Afghanistan. Many have died. Nine years is a long time."

DIFFERENT WAR, SAME SITUATION
NINE YEARS LATER, AFGHAN CITY IS BUZZING BUT STILL MENACING
AUGUST 20, 2010

Taloqan, Afghanistan—Nine years ago, when I was using this provincial Afghan capital as a base to cover the battle of Kunduz,

Taloqan was a dangerous place with medieval charm. Donkey carts and horse-drawn carriages were pervasive. The steeds decked out with red pom-poms plied muddy ruts that passed as roads. The only motorized transport belonged to Western NGOs. Commerce consisted of a few sad huts you'd recognize as primitive convenience stores and an outdoor bazaar where 90 percent of economic activity was attributable to sales of opium paste.

In 2001 I wrote that good roads would change everything. And they have. Sometime after 2005, when *The New York Times* reported that the United States hadn't laid an inch of pavement in the entire country, road building happened—at least here in Takhar and in neighboring Kunduz province.

The ghosts of '01 are here—burned-out armored personnel carriers, lumps of earth where villages stood, tank treads used as speed bumps—but hard to find. Khanabad, the blood-soaked eastern front line during the battle of Kunduz, where my fellow journalist had the skin torn off his body by Taliban POWs using their bare hands, is a farm community marked by the kind of green-and-white reflectorized sign you'd see in the Midwest.

Most of Taloqan is paved. The donkeys and horses are gone. The soccer field used by the Taliban for stonings and by a Northern Alliance warlord as a helicopter landing pad is filled with kids playing on green grass. There are traffic jams (of cars and Indian-style motorized rickshaws) and white-gloved traffic cops to direct the mayhem. Business is booming. America is finished, but Taloqan is looking good.

Asphalt made a difference. But the basics—the social and political situation that in December 2001 prompted me to declare the U.S. occupation of Afghanistan doomed—remain the same.

Time magazine recently declared that the Taliban would sweep back into power after a U.S. withdrawal, brutalizing the women and stuffing them back under burqas. But the Taliban never left. Neither

Afghans love to pimp their rides.

did the repression. In Taloqan every woman but one wore the burqa, turning her head away so we couldn't see her eyes through the netting as we passed.

Where are the Taliban? "They are all around us," said my driver's cousin, the campaign manager for a Canadian Afghan actor running for parliament next month. "During the day, it is okay. They come at night."

Indeed they do. The week before our arrival they stormed a small NATO garrison staffed by German troops at the airport here, killing seven. Cellphone signals go dead at night in deference to Taliban strictures.

Money is exchanging hands. But the one thing Afghans wanted most in 2001—security—remains elusive. Though it is not a historical novelty, it is ironic that people are turning to those who create the threat in order to resolve it.

FOUR: THE SECOND BATTLE OF KUNDUZ

The Afghan government is the lawful government. But the Taliban's law is the gun.
—Abdul Wahed Omarkhiel, quoted in *The Washington Post*, 2010. Omarkhiel is head of the Chardara district, four miles from Kunduz.

I t's not every day that you get to sit in a roomful of Afghans who speak English. How did these young men, these English tutors, feel about the United States? I wanted to know. How was the security situation? Were they generally hopeful or pessimistic?

"The number one problem is security," one said. We heard this throughout Afghanistan. "The Taliban are everywhere. They come and go as they please."

And the government of Hamid Karzai?

The Afghans we asked split into rough thirds about the U.S.-appointed president. These points of view could be summarized as follows:

"He is a good man, but he is too weak to do anything."

"He is no one. Afghans don't care about him."

"Kill him."

No one thought he was an effective leader. No one held hope that he would curb corruption or provide security at any point in the future. Afghans were staring into the abyss. The neo-Taliban would be in charge sooner rather than later. Some people didn't like it, but every-one accepted—and expected—it.

Our driver, who'd originally offered to take us the rest of our jour-ney, tried to shake us down for a higher fee when he heard we were heading to Mazar-i-Sharif. We had no choice. The only road west passes through Kunduz. Otherwise it's north to Tajikistan or east to the remote mountains of the Wakhan Corridor.

We agreed. But then, faced with the reality of passing through Taliban-controlled Kunduz with three Americans, he decided to pass. This was sobering. Afghanistan's poverty is brutal; the kind of money we were offering far surpassed anything else he'd ever be able to get. He could only be refusing for one reason: terror.

We scared up a replacement and headed off. "I will not stop in Kunduz for anything," he warned. "I will drive very fast through there. I do not care if you must use the toilet, I will not stop there. Taliban, Taliban everywhere there," he said. We agreed.

We zoomed through Khanabad, site of the main battlefront in 2001. Again, I marveled at the contrast. In '01 we knew we were in Khanabad because people told us. Now there's an official white-on-blue sign marking the entrance of town. In '01 the road was not only unpaved, but downright medieval; now it's smooth blacktop.

As we drove west, I scanned the horizon in search of the blast cra-ter left by the daisy cutter bomb. It was gone. So was the neighborhood it had destroyed. It was as if it had never existed. There were no ruins, no shattered walls, no caved-in roofs. Afghanistan's abject poverty has an upside from an environmental standpoint: everything gets reused. People had salvaged the site for bricks and wooden beams.

In '01, Khanabad marked Taliban lines. Today the formal battlefield is, of course, no more. The fields around Khanabad are lush; red flags left by demining teams indicate the area is safe to cultivate, and that's exactly what we saw people doing. Khanabad has all the outward signs of a vibrant farming town.

Yet, in some ways, things are the same.

The Taliban still control the region west of Khanabad. No one stopped us, but we could tell. Recently wrecked oil tankers, burned black, lined the side of the highway. Blast marks on the asphalt served as mute testimony to the Taliban's relentless campaign to deprive of fuel the Karzai government and the businesses whose mere existence classified them as traitors. There were still government machine gun nests every few miles, but in the Taliban zone they were more often than not unmanned or occupied so lackadaisically that they had might as well be vacant. Afghan cops slept on cots out front or on the roofs.

Our driver nervously scanned the horizon. I asked him what he was looking for.

"Motorcycles," he said. "The Taliban come on motorcycles."

As I'd packed for Afghanistan I was reading everything I could about the country and the war. As our driver talked, my mind flashed to an article I'd read about a round of classified government documents, the so-called Afghan War Diary, which was published by the website WikiLeaks in July 2010. The Diary had focused on Pakistan's double game; armed and funded by the United States to the tune of billions of dollars annually, its intelligence services funneled much of the cash to their allies, the Taliban—who used it to kill U.S. troops. One memo, from 2007, had drawn my eye: Pakistani intelligence had given a thousand motorbikes to the Haqqani network, a terrorist organization aligned with the Taliban that controls North Waziristan in the Tribal Areas along the Pakistani-Afghan border, for suicide attacks in the Khost and Logar provinces in Afghanistan.

Motorbikes? I remember wondering. How odd. Suicide attacks, however, were only the beginning. The Taliban used Afghan-made Pamir-brand dirtbikes to form mobile strike forces that transformed northern Afghanistan, dominated by non-Pashtun tribes and thus considered "stable" and "safe" by Afghan government analysts and their U.S. allies, into a free-fire zone.

I dubbed this new phenomenon the Talibikers. They were the highly adaptable neo-Taliban response to the Afghan government gun nests. Rather than set up permanent or semipermanent checkpoints along the roads that could be attacked by drones or conventional fighter jets, the Talibikers were based in small villages anywhere from ten to thirty kilometers from the highway.

Joshua Partlow, who was encountering these Taliban bike gangs a couple of hundred kilometers ahead of us at that time, wrote in *The Washington Post* a few days later: "In squads of roaring dirt bikes and armed to the teeth, Taliban fighters are spreading like a brush fire into remote and defenseless villages across northern Afghanistan. The fighters swarm into town, assemble the villagers, and announce Taliban control, often at night and without any resistance. They move constantly on unmarked dirt roads outside the cities to ambush Afghan police and soldiers and to kidnap residents. They execute those affiliated with the government and shut down reconstruction projects. They plant homemade bombs, close girls' schools, and take by force a portion of farmers' crops and residents' salaries."

The Talibikers hadn't given up on checkpoints. They would sweep across the desert, intercept vehicles at impromptu checkpoints, then vanish before dusk. The fates of those ensnared by their raids depended on their whims. Fuel truck drivers and government workers were executed. Small businessmen, traders, and their wives would usually be shaken down for cash. In an ironic twist (the Taliban had initially

AFGHANISTAN'S TALIBAN MOVEMENT, LIKE ANY UNDERGROUND
RESISTANCE GROUP, MUST CONSTANTLY ADAPT TO CHANGING CONDITIONS.
INNOVATION CAN DETERMINE WHETHER VICTORY OR DEFEAT ENSUES. AND
SO THEY'VE COME UP WITH A NEW TACTIC. IT'S RIGHT OUT OF A 1970s
EXPLOITATION MOVIE. THINK "MAD MAX," OR:

TALIBAN BIKE GANGS FROM HELL

A SEEMINGLY CALM
LATE AFTERNOON IN
WESTERN FARYAB PROVINCE

TALIBAN,
SCHLALIBAN

HAW

BUT THEN—

EMERGING FROM THE DESERT LIKE AVENGING
ANGELS, TALIBAN BIKERS ON AFGHAN-MADE
PAMIR MOTORBIKES ZERO IN ON THEIR HAPLESS PREY.

FASTER!

THEY'RE
GAINING!

TALIBAN BIKE GANGS NOW
EFFECTIVELY CONTROL SOUTHERN
KUNDUZ AND BALKH PROVINCES,
AS WELL AS ALL OF FARYAB AND
BAGHLIS.

BASED IN THE RURAL AREAS AWAY FROM
HIGHWAYS GUARDED BY GOVERNMENT
GUN NESTS EVERY FEW KILOMETERS,
TALIBIKERS STRIKE WITH LIGHTNING
SPEED AND ESCAPE WITH IMPUNITY.

I'M WAITING FOR ROBT. RODRÍGUEZ AND QUENTIN TARANTINO TO OPTION THE RIGHTS.

come to power as defenders of women's honor and killed rapists), women were at risk of gang rape.

The cold truth was that the U.S. military could easily have put a stop to the Talibikers. Unlike the Afghan wedding parties mistakenly targeted by Predator drones, there is no doubt, even from ten thousand feet up, about the intentions of two hundred dirtbikers speeding across the Afghan desert toward a convoy of fuel trucks in a remote area of a backwater province. It would be easy to kill them.

Alas, no one tried. It became rapidly evident that U.S. and NATO war aims in Afghanistan did not include providing security to the Afghan people. They were barely interested in engaging Taliban forces in combat, even when they were ambushed by them. The real war was in Pakistan and in a narrow band of territory in Afghanistan along the Pakistan border. The men and women stationed at Bagram airbase weren't there to occupy Afghanistan. They used Afghanistan as a staging ground to attack Taliban targets well inside Pakistan.

There was no Afghan war. The United States values and covets Pakistan as a strategic counterbalance to China and India and the linchpin of relations between the two. Americans fought in Afghanistan, lost limbs and minds and some died, but their sacrifice and that of the Afghans they killed were about securing a launching pad for drones and fighter jets.

"I must stop here," our driver informed us. Just inside Kunduz.

Typically Afghan. He had insisted, begged even, that we zip through Taliban-infested Kunduz, no stops, no excuses, no exceptions. "If you need to use the bathroom," he helpfully pointed out, "use water bottle." Which was fine with us. By all accounts, the Karzai regime and NATO were close to nonexistent there. We'd been prepared to hunker down under our scarves and look relaxed as we zipped through town.

What the hell?

"There is a problem with the car," he said. "We must stop." We

couldn't hear anything. Was he lying? We couldn't communicate car talk.

Was he about to sell us to the Taliban? Matt, Steven, and I didn't discuss it; everyone understood that acting scared would only make things worse, and besides, we were so parched from not drinking for hours due to Ramadan that it hurt to talk. But, as we discussed later, we knew there was no point arguing. It wasn't like we could get out and hail another cab. Once you put yourself at the mercy of a local driver or guide, there wasn't much you could do if he decided to betray you. All you could do is trust your initial instincts and hope for the best.

Inshallah.

We hung a left onto Jada-i-Mawlawi Samajuddin, passed the police station—no cops anywhere, ominous—and swung right down a narrow alley. Matt, Steven, and I looked at one another. This seemed sketchy. Not that we stood much of a chance out on the main drag, but this was a cul-de-sac. Nowhere to go.

Noon. Blazing hot.

Pedestrians stared at us. Some glared. Were they crabby permafrown people, or badass Talibs? Our car emerged into an enclosed plaza. Along the edges were storefront shacks selling auto-repair-related merchandise: tires, belts, tubes, etc. We pulled up to one. "Do not move," our driver told us. "Do not leave the car. If anyone talks to you, pretend to be stupid. Do not say anything."

If there's anything I know how to do, it's act stupid.

We slouched into our seats, wrapped our scarves around our heads tighter, getting thirstier and hotter by the minute as the sun hit high noon. No cheating on Ramadan here while everyone was watching. Thirsty and sweltering, we kept as still as possible, sweat glistening, even between our fingers. Every now and then someone would slip into a hole under the car, bang something, and come out. People walked

Street scene, Mazar-i-Sharif

by, looked at us. Some talked to us. Wild eyes, big beards, craggy faces. Anger? Couldn't tell.

We ignored them. *Act stupid.*

Cellphones everywhere. "Look at that kid," Steven said, indicating a boy, about twelve, yakking on a phone near a grimy stack of pistons as he stared at us. "Think he wouldn't sell us out to the Taliban for ten afghanis?" There was nothing to do but wait. Time crawled.

The Taliban could have come for us at any time during those two hours of waiting. No one would have cared. Certainly no one would have stopped them, not even us. But they didn't. Finally, we felt something snap into place under the car. A few whacks of a hammer. Metal on metal.

Our driver reappeared. Smiling, he handed a few thousand afghani notes to a boy. Got in, not a word to us, but we knew he wasn't going to betray us.

Maybe there weren't any buyers.

The highway to Mazar was littered with the detritus of more vehicles blown up by IEDs. It wasn't tough to guess that we were driving by countless roadside bombs, many of them monitored by sharp-eyed guerrilla fighters watching from behind rocks and trees. We were the

Soviet-era tanks still litter the countryside.

twitch of a thumb away from oblivion. All we had to do was look like people they didn't like.

It was a cool, balmy one hundred twenty-five degrees in Mazar-i-Sharif, the biggest city I had seen in Afghanistan. I liked it. Afghanistan's second-largest city was hot and dusty, very Central Asian. Big and sprawling, it felt like the kind of place where you could get lost. In a good way: it was big enough, with a big enough variety of people that you felt like you might not get noticed by the wrong sorts. Unfortunately, it didn't have a lot of exciting architecture or natural beauty. Sort of like Los Angeles, it's just a sprawling place where a lot of people happen to live at the same time.

A city of mostly three-story buildings laid out across a sprawling plain, it differed from Kunduz and Taloqan mainly in size, not cosmopolitanism (although, as we soon observed, it was home to a population of young male hipsters). Unlike in Western countries, where large cities have decidedly different character than smaller ones, Afghan cities, including Kabul, have all the same basic kinds of businesses and architecture as small provincial ones. They simply have more of them.

Unlike Taloqan, there were several hotels catering to foreigners. All charged outrageous prices for inferior accommodations. We drove around, looked at rooms, haggled, and eventually settled on a newish joint built by the Soviets, which I found somehow comforting. Electricity was on offer for stretches of time; whenever it came on we rushed to turn on the air conditioner, charge up our electronic devices, and check email. It even had wifi.

We settled into a routine. We woke up early, went out to do outside stuff (hang out at a local mosque, interview people, see the sights) in the morning, and spent the afternoons inside hiding from the sun, drawing, writing, and reading.

In an echo of 2001, when I'd read *Anna Karenina*, I brought Tolstoy's *War and Peace*. Not as good, I thought, but still great. In late afternoon—we didn't want to get caught outside at dark—we'd go out in search of food. One of the hotels we'd rejected as too expensive had an expat restaurant-bar, formerly called the Royal Oak, now nameless. As we notified people back home via social networking sites: "We are drinking the only beers in Afghanistan." Obviously not the only ones. But it felt that way. Even though they were lukewarm, we felt like kings.

Stephanie McMillan had agreed to serve as our news lifeline back home. Armed with our itinerary and latest status updates, she would scour the Web for news about Afghanistan in general and the specific regions we were going to next. In one such report she forwarded us Josh Partlow's worrisome article from the *Post*. Filed from Faryab province, it asserted that the northern ring road between Mazar and Herat was overrun with Talibikers who liked to kidnap foreigners and hold them for insanely high ransoms. There was no government presence there to speak of.

Jama Masjid (Great Mosque), Herat

Shrine of Hazrat Ali (Blue Mosque), Mazar-i-Sharif

Ted, Matt, and Steven, Mazar-i-Sharif. It was 122 degrees.

YOU TRAVEL OVERSEAS TO IMMERSE YOURSELF IN NEW AND DIFFERENT CULTURES. THAT INCLUDES FOOD. SOMETIMES, HOWEVER, YOU FIND YOURSELF LONGING FOR THE COMFORT OF FAMILIAR TASTES. SO YOU SEEK OUT

AFGHAN VERSIONS OF AMERICAN FOOD

NO FOOD GETS MORE ATTEMPTS AT AFGHANIZATION THAN PIZZA. FROM TOPPINGS TO CONDIMENTS, THE RESULTS RANGE FROM STRANGE TO SCARY.

"FISH" (AFGHANISTAN IS FAMOUSLY LANDLOCKED)

CHICKEN (WITH BONE IN)

OKRA

LAMB CURRY

RANDOM GLOOPY MASS OF RED MYSTERY SAUCE (NOT TOMATO)

CRUST FROZEN SINCE PALEOLITHIC TIMES

ALL AFGHAN PIZZA JOINTS PROVIDE THESE CONDIMENTS WITH YOUR MEAL:

BECAUSE AFGHANS REALLY HAVE TO WATCH THEIR WAISTLINES!

Light Mayonnaise Sauce

TOMATO KETSUP DIET

DON'T MISS HERAT'S FAMOUS
BURGER TUBE!

10"

BOTTOM BUN: POPPY   TOP BUN: PLAIN

VAGUELY GAMEY MYSTERY MEAT (CAMEL? HORSE? ROADKILL DOG?)

LOTS AND LOTS O' LITE MAYO!!!

THINK YOU CAN'T GO WRONG WITH A HARD-BOILED EGG? **WRONG!** 2 OUT OF 3 CONTAIN UNIDENTIFIABLE **BLACK SPOTS**

SHOULD I EAT IT?

NO. IT'S AN EGG.

IT SMELLS TOO.

Approach to the Salang Tunnel

I emailed Josh. He was safely out of Afghanistan, but he strongly cautioned against our plan to drive through Qaysar, the town where he'd nearly gotten detained by Talibikers.

We discussed our options over spaghetti and mantu at the Royal Oak.

"The *Post* story is several days old," I pointed out. "Maybe we should stick to the original plan [to hire a driver to take us west to Herat, via the Uzbek stronghold of Maimana]."

"Maimana is where they play *buzkashi*," Matt said. *Buzkashi*, or "goat bashing" in Turkic, is horse polo played with the exsanguinated headless body of a goat. Popular through Central Asia, the Mongol sport is notable for its lack of rules. Anything goes, including whipping and stabbing rivals. Gunplay is not unknown; it is frowned upon but not considered illegal. Maimings and deaths are common in the world's most violent sport.

OPPOSITE: **Heading south on the A76 highway through the Hindu Kush**

Matt really wanted to see *buzkashi*.

"We're not sure there will even be a match at this time of year," I said truthfully. "It's mostly during the spring." I liked that our blood-lust was part of the calculus over whether or not to risk our lives.

"There's another option," I said. We could drive south to Kabul, then turn west toward Herat via the so-called Central Route over the Hindu Kush. I unfolded one of the maps and laid it across the table. "There are no reports of violence along the Central Route. But we'd have to go through the Salang Tunnel."

We finished our canned beers and made our way out to the street. It was dark. Dark was bad.

We tried to hail a passing car. No one stopped. Of course: it was night. We were afraid; so was everyone else. After half an hour a familiar car pulled up: our driver. The owner of the restaurant came outside. "I called your hotel and told them to send him." He smiled. A minor gesture. But such consideration is exceedingly rare. Hell, it may have saved our lives. Foreigners can't just hang out on the streets of Afghan cities, especially at night. He refused a tip.

Maybe things were going to be okay.

THE SHRINE OF HAZRAT ALI IS ONE OF THE MOST CELEBRATED TOURIST ATTRACTIONS IN AFGHANISTAN.

MAZAR-I-SHARIF, BALKH PROVINCE

BUT THE SHRINE'S MUSEUM IS A SAD AFFAIR — REFLECTING, NO DOUBT, THE CONSTANT DESTRUCTION OF AFGHANISTAN'S CULTURAL PATRIMONY.

Holy Koran (Qu'ran), Tiny, Century 11, British

Gift from Turkmenistan

Thing made from mud Century 3

HOWEVER, IT ISN'T WITHOUT ITS CHARMS.

A FARMER FOUND THIS COW. LOOK — IT HAS **ALLAH'S NAME** ON IT!

AMAZING.

THE MUSEUM HAS A WHOLE SECTION DEDICATED TO THE MIRACULOUS APPEARANCE OF ALLAH'S NAME ON UNLIKELY ORGANIC ITEMS.

Beet

Someone's Eye

Bread

IT'S EXACTLY THE SAME AS THOSE STORIES ABOUT JESUS APPEARING ON A TACO OR THE VIRGIN MARY IN A SLICE OF PIZZA.

BEHOLD!

FINALLY, COMMON GROUND THAT WILL END THE CLASH OF CIVILIZATIONS:

REALLY? YOU SAW THE PROPHET IN A MARSHMALLOW?

YES — AND HE WAS BOWLING WITH JESUS!

STUPIDITY.

THE BAD NEWS ABOUT FOOD IN AFGHANISTAN IS THAT IT'S GODAWFUL.

Trying to Balance on Squat Toilet

Day 3: Diarrhea o' doom

THE GOOD NEWS IS, THERE ISN'T MUCH OF IT.

BUT IT'S GOT ITS GOOD POINTS TOO.

Mutton Kebabs — One piece of fat per skewer

Mantu (Mystery Dumplings)

Nan Bread ⅓ Watery Chai

Afghan Staples

THE MAIN THING IS: FOOD TASTES LIKE **FOOD**, NOT INDUSTRIALLY MANUFACTURED, DUBIOUSLY PRESERVED FOOD PRODUCT.

Apples that are juicy and rich, not mealy and flavorless

Possible worm hole — Whatever. Eat around it!

Watermelons came from Central Asia. I hate 'em in the U.S.— not here.

Chicken that's gamey and delish

ON THE <u>OTHER</u> OTHER HAND, IT'S RAMADAN. SINCE IT'S UNSAFE TO GO OUT AT NIGHT— THE ONLY TIME RESTAURANTS ARE OPEN—WE HAVE TO SNEAK FOOD AND WATER OR HAVE IT DELIVERED BY THE STAFF AT OUR GUESTHOUSE.

CARBONATED NEON-GREEN SUGAR WATER NEVER TASTED SO GOOD!

Mountain Dew from Dubai

FORBIDDEN FRUIT AND ALL THAT...

THE HIPSTERS OF MAZAR

AFGHAN CLOTHING IS AS COOKIE-CUTTER AS IT GETS:

WOMEN		MEN
FORMAL	CASUAL	

Scarf (also serves as blanket)

Vest (optional variation: photographer-style pocket vest from China)

Shalwar Kameez

Headgear varies:
Other options:

SKULLCAP

Pakul*

* Popularized by Northern Alliance, widespread in 2001. Now hardly ever seen.

BUT SOME YOUNG URBAN MEN ARE DITCHING THE UBIQUITOUS <u>SHALWAR</u> <u>KAMEEZ</u> IN FAVOR OF TIGHT, WESTERN-STYLE, USUALLY LOGO-FESTOONED CLOTHING.

Even skinnier than the average, crazy skinny Afghan dudes

THESE SNOTTY REBELS SCOFF AT TRADITION. AS OTHERS SUFFER THE LONG DAYS OF RAMADAN WITHOUT FOOD OR DRINK, THEY FLOUT CONVENTION— AND RELIGIOUS NORMS— BY OPENLY GUZZLING WATER.

Internet sez it's 85°
Thermometer sez 110°+

WHY DO THEY BUCK AUTHORITY? WHO KNOWS. EVEN IF I KNEW, I'D JUST HAVE MORE QUESTIONS. LIKE: IT'S RAMADAN. SO WHY IS HOT FOOD AND ICE-COLD DRINK AVAILABLE DURING THE DAY?

It's on offer. But it's haram.* So who's buying?

*Forbidden

TODAY'S LESSON:
TAXI CAB DIARY, MAZAR-I-SHARIF EDITION.

FYI:

 =

$1 = 50 afghanis

(unless your money changer gives you 40 because "America is down today")

HAZRAT ALI? [SOMETHING IN DARI]

4 fingers indicating 40-afghani fare

3 fingers, indicating 30-afghani counteroffer

THE DRIVER NODDED, AGREEING TO 30 AFGHANIS.

BUT:

NÉ NÉ! Demanding 50-afghani fare

WE OFFER THE 40 AFGHANIS HE WANTED ORIGINALLY.

BUT HE REFUSES! HE'S FURIOUS. HE TAKES THE 40 AFGHANIS AND THROWS THEM AT US!

"Get out of my car" shooing-away gesture

HE'S SO PISSED OFF, WE GET SCARED AND PAY HIM 50 — MORE THAN HE WANTED TO BEGIN WITH.

WHOA — HE'S REFUSING MONEY?!

HERE YOU GO. OK? OK?

20¢ ISN'T WORTH MAKING ANYONE — ESPECIALLY AN AFGHAN — ANGRY.

IT'S ELECTION SEASON. WHICH IS GOOD FOR THE POSTER-PRINTING BUSINESS.

AT LEAST 90% OF PUBLIC ADVERTISING IN AFGHANISTAN IS FOR POLITICAL CANDIDATES.

THE REST IS FOR CELLPHONE COMPANIES.

AMERICAN POLITICIANS ALWAYS SMILE. NOT AFGHANS. THEY AFFECT A SOMBER, SERIOUS, DIGNIFIED TONE.

1 ONLY SAW ONE WITH A HAND VISIBLE. HE WAS POINTING.

A SIGNIFICANT PROPORTION OF CANDIDATES ARE FEMALE — FAR MORE THAN IN THE UNITED STATES. THEY LOOK BEYOND SERIOUS. THEY'RE DOUR. SOURPUSSES, EVEN.

SORT OF HOW REPUBLICANS LIKE TO EVOKE REAGAN, MANY HARKEN BACK TO AHMED SHAH MASSOUD, THE CHARISMATIC NORTHERN ALLIANCE GENERAL ASSASSINATED BY AL QAEDA 2 DAYS BEFORE 9/11.

Double Massouds!!

THEY PHOTOSHOP MASSOUD'S PHOTO IN NEXT TO THEIRS.

"Lion of the Panjshir" (Dead)

WHETHER THE IDEA IS TO IMPLY THAT MASSOUD WOULD ENDORSE THEM (WERE HE STILL ALIVE) OR THAT THEY LIKE MASSOUD'S POLITICS, THE EFFECT IS DECIDEDLY CREEPY.

MANY AFGHANS ARE ILLITERATE.

Cheesy uniforms issued to Afghan National Police hurt their pride

"TED"? THIS IS REAL NAME?

holding passport upside down

SO, AS A CONCESSION TO THE LOW LEVEL OF EDUCATION, AFGHAN CANDIDATES INCLUDE SOME EASY-TO-REMEMBER SYMBOLIC GRAPHIC ON THEIR POSTERS... WHICH WILL APPEAR NEXT TO THEIR NAME ON THE BALLOT.

TWO CHERRIES

BECAUSE THERE ARE SO MANY MEN AND WOMEN RUNNING FOR PARLIAMENT, THE CHOICES OF ICON CAN GET PRETTY ESOTERIC. YOU CAN'T HELP WONDERING:

Would the Islamist-looking fellow running for MP rather have something more masculine?

Does the laptop logo mean this chap is forward-looking?

I IMAGINE THEM SHOOTING SNIDE COMMENTS AND INSULTS ABOUT ONE ANOTHER'S SYMBOLS IN DEBATES:

YER GONNA NEED THEM 2 WHEELBARROWS TO HAUL YOUR LOSING BUTT BACK TO YOUR HICK PROVINCE!

4 LIGHTBULBS... BUT NOT ONE NEW IDEA!

NOT ALL SYMBOLS ARE EQUALLY MEMORABLE. OR APPEALING. I DON'T KNOW THAT I'D WANT TO RUN A CAMPAIGN THAT DEPENDED ON VOTERS TURNING OUT FOR THE "3 PISTACHIOS" GUY.

@★#! DUDE PULLS STRINGS AND GETS A FRIGGIN'

CHANGE OF PLAN.

HM.

Mazar guesthouse ↓

A *WASHINGTON POST* ARTICLE FILED MERELY 2 DAYS BEFORE OUR PLANNED DEPARTURE TO MAIMANA INDICATES THE ENTIRE PROVINCE HAS BEEN OVERRUN WITH BRAZEN TALIBAN BIKER BANDITS.

WE COULD GO TO MAIMANA, THEN TURN SOUTH OVER THE 12,000-FT. PASS TOWARD THE CENTRAL ROUTE.

OR WE CAN JUST TAKE THE CENTRAL ROUTE!

AN EMAIL FROM ITS AUTHOR CONFIRMS: THESE GUYS DON'T LIKE JOURNALISTS.

WE DON'T CARE ABOUT MAIMANA. WE CARE ABOUT HERAT—WE WANT TO SEE IF THERE'S A PIPELINE. WE CAN GET THERE IF WE GO TO KABUL FIRST.

IT WAS.

BUT YOU SAID THE SALANG TUNNEL AREA WAS BAD.

MONTHS AGO, WHEN I RESEARCHED THE TRIP, THE SALANG TUNNEL ON THE KABUL-TO-MAZAR HIGHWAY WAS DANGEROUS. SO INSTEAD OF FLYING INTO KABUL, WE WENT INTO DUSHANBE AND DROVE TO TALOQAN AND THEN MAZAR.

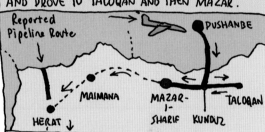

Reported Pipeline Route

DUSHANBE

MAIMANA

MAZAR-I-SHARIF   KUNDUZ   TALOQAN

HERAT ↓

BACK THEN, NORTHERN AFGHANISTAN WAS QUIET. BUT NOW THE HIGHWAY FROM MAZAR TO HERAT HAS BECOME IMPASSABLE. WE HAVE TO MODIFY OUR BEST-LAID PLAN.

MAIMANA

SAR-E HOWZ

HERE BE TALIBAN

HERAT

WE'RE NOT SCARED OF THE TALIBAN. BUT ROBBERS WOULD END OUR JOURNEY. SO WE AGREE ON THE **CENTRAL ROUTE** TO HERAT.

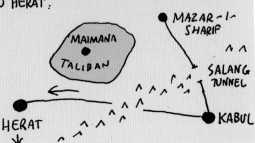

MAIMANA TALIBAN

MAZAR-I-SHARIF

SALANG TUNNEL

HERAT ↓

KABUL

THE SALANG TUNNEL IS A MARVEL OF ENGINEERING. IT IS THE KEY STRATEGIC LINK BETWEEN NORTHERN AND SOUTHERN AFGHANISTAN.

"Pillbox" for Machine-gun nest

BUILT BY THE SOVIET UNION DURING THE LATE 1950s AND 1960s, THE TUNNEL IS BENEATH THE SALANG PASS AT 11,200 FT. IT IS 1.6 MILES LONG.

Mazar-i-Sharif

HINDU KUSH* MOUNTAINS

Kabul

*"Killer of Hindus"

DURING THE CIVIL WAR THAT BEGAN IN 1979, THE TUNNEL WAS BOMBED, SABOTAGED, AND THE SITE OF PITCHED BATTLES. IT WAS ALSO MINED. THE ONLY WAY IT COULD BE CROSSED WAS ON FOOT IN THE DARK.

NOW THE WRECKAGE AND MINES AND CORPSES ARE GONE. BUT IT'S STILL A FRIGHTENING, SPOOKY EXPERIENCE.

THE BOTTOM OF THE TUNNEL IS UNPAVED MUD. WHICH COMES FROM LEAKS. BECAUSE THE TUNNEL ISN'T SEALED. WHICH IS WHY CONCRETE SUPPORTS HAVE ERODED AND COLLAPSED.

Rebar

THAT CAN'T BE GOOD

Nightlight-strength lamps

AFGHANS TREAT THE TUNNEL LIKE ANY ORDINARY ROAD. THEY PASS IN 3s IN LANES FOR 2, WEAVE AROUND EACH OTHER RANDOMLY.

THE TERROR THEY CREATE NORMALIZES THE FEAR INHERENT TO THE LOCATION.

FIVE: KABUL, CITY OF BLAST WALLS

If you're thinking about taking a yoga class at Kabul's Fig Health Centre, you'll be relieved to know that the yoga studio windows are packed with tilting stacks of green sandbags. That way, if a car bomb goes off during yoga class, the sandbags and anti-blast glass will offer a little extra protection from flying shrapnel.

—from "Yoga, Blast Walls and Life in the Afghan 'Kabubble,'" by Dion Nissenbaum, *McClatchy Newspapers*, July 15, 2010

Thank the movies. When you drive into Kabul from the north, the view is every bit as iconic as the Manhattan skyline: one- and two-story mudbrick houses forming an amphitheater of misery up the incline of matching brown mountains. You've seen them in *The Kite Runner* and on the evening news. Millions of slum-dwelling Kabulis have a million-afghani view of history being made in the smoggy punchbowl below.

We passed the old Hotel Intercontinental, where in 2001 a correspondent for the Knight-Ridder newspaper chain had gone mad from fear (whether of the Taliban or U.S. bombs, no one could say) and had to be extracted, in the words of his replacement, "tied to a board."

"Fucking little crybaby," the new Knight-Ridder guy groused over what passed for breakfast the morning of the day we'd entered Afghanistan in 2001. "Crying for his mama." He looked up at me and didn't like what he saw. A smirk, no doubt.

Wazir Akbar Khan neighborhood, Kabul

Trudging into the lobby of the Hotel Tajikistan, the remains of our convoy had been like a defeated army. Starved, terrorized, and end-lessly banged around (and of course covered with dust, dust, so much dust that it was still coming out my ears a month later), we dropped our luggage and gear on the marble floors in a last release as exhaus-

tion replaced fading tension. A Frenchwoman, a reporter in her forties, too elegant for Central Asia and certainly for Afghanistan, was preparing to go in the next convoy. She asked me—people always ask me questions, I have one of those faces—

"What is the situation in Afghanistan?"

I didn't know what to say. So I didn't.

"Don't go," a woman from Bulgarian TV behind me advised. "Go back to your room. Tomorrow morning go to the airport. Get on the plane. Go back to Paris. Enjoy your life."

Ignoring her, the Frenchwoman got up into my face. "But what is the *situation*?"

I pointed to the coffin. "That. That is the situation," I said.

Sure, 99.99 percent of foreigners who go to Afghanistan come home alive, all limbs still attached and functional. But it didn't feel that way in 2001. Not for us. Our odds had been much worse: 42 out of 45 alive, or 14 in 15. Or 36 out of 45 basically intact . . . about three out of four.

Across the traffic circle from the Intercontinental, rolls of razor wire and an armored pillbox bearing the sign RING OF STEEL marked the entrance of Kabul proper. I'd heard about this. Karzai had ordered the placement of twenty-five Afghan National Police checkpoints at all the entrances to the capital to protect it from Taliban attacks. It had been a few months. Now the pillboxes were unmanned.

It hadn't gotten safer. To the contrary: everyone we talked to, Afghans and foreigners alike, agreed that the Taliban were basically running most of the country and could come and go as they pleased in the urban pockets still under government control. But vigilance is boring.

The situation was different in 2010. Possibly because Mullah Omar, head of the Islamic Emirate of Afghanistan, aka the Taliban, alternatively referred to as chief of the Shura of Quetta, where he lives relatively openly, had ordered that journalists be allowed to work unmolested, reporters were no longer being hunted for sport. Of course, all bets were off if you traveled with American or NATO troops as an "embed." Then you were considered a spy, propagandist for the occupation, and therefore fair game. I can't say that I disagree with their reasoning—if it were my country I'd feel the same way.

The three of us discussed the safety issue. The truth is, it's always a guess as to whether a particular area is safe or not. If lots of foreigners go to a place and nothing happens for a while, it acquires a good reputation. If there's an attack, however, the same place instantly becomes terrifying. This is what happened in July, shortly before our arrival. Ten people working for a Swiss Christian medical charity, the International Assistance Mission, were shot to death by the Taliban in Badakhshan, a province in the northeast that is the most remote part of the country. Badakhshan, previously considered calm, was suddenly considered off-limits for foreigners. At this writing, however, there have

Two of the countless private security guards, Kabul

been no more major incidents. If this keeps up, foreigners will go back to Badakhshan.

The main dangers to reporters in 2010 were kidnapping and robbery, either of which could easily lead to murder. We figured we wouldn't be kidnapped. We weren't working for a major media outlet that might be shaken down for large sums of money. Also, we were a target that was constantly in motion. From what we'd read, Afghan kidnappers shadow their victims for days before making their move. We didn't plan to be in any one place more than a day or two.

Robbery was the big concern. It was virtually impossible to get anywhere without money. Arrive at a checkpoint without bribe money, and you might never leave.

On the other hand, the cell service was excellent. Much better than Long Island, New York, where I live. As it turned out, I didn't need most of the gear I lugged with me. I hardly ever used the solar panels. The sat phone was nice to have in case of emergency, especially in rural areas, but the most useful electronic device to have in Afghanistan is

Store destroyed by a suicide bomber, Kabul

an ordinary smartphone outfitted with an Afghan SIM card to make cheap local calls. Number two was a GPS tracking device with a panic button to use in case of, say, a kidnapping.

Kabul is a city of five million people. But you don't see them. You see blast walls and AK-toting security guards. Every block has some facility that might be targeted by the neo-Taliban: embassies, NGOs, schools, hospitals, hotels, guesthouses, stores. Here the Middle Ages have been updated to a new age of feudal insecurity and political disorder.

We stayed at a traditional journalists' hangout near Sherpur Square, the Gandamack Lodge. Owned by a British war cameraman, Peter Jouvenal, the Gandamack had previously served as an Al Qaeda safe-house and as living quarters of Osama bin Laden's fourth wife and family. We found a pleasant garden, including one marijuana plant growing in a pot in front of Steven's room, an Egyptian correspondent for Al Jazeera who made regular runs to war-torn Helmand province in a burqa, a couple dozen sleazy "contractors" (i.e., mercenaries) and underpaid, overdressed Afghan waitstaff. The highlight of life at the

Afghan policeman. Their uniforms do not elicit respect.

Gandamack was the evening, when there was beer. As I watched tawdry romances unfold between fiftyish mercs and twentysomething NGO workers, I noticed the disapproving glances of the Afghans. Parallels with 1839, when the Brits invaded Kabul and indulged in behavior that scandalized Afghans (mainly alcohol and licentiousness), were hard not to think about. By 1842, all but one of the British party boys had been massacred.

Dust storm, Kabul

As if the colonial-era weaponry wasn't enough to evoke that "signal disaster," as the nineteenth-century press called it, there's that name. The Gandamack Treaty, signed on the same site in 1879, ended the Second Anglo-Afghan War with the humiliating cession of a swath of Afghan border regions to the British Raj.

I assumed that a job at the Gandamack would be a plum gig for an Afghan. After all, we were paying one hundred sixty-five dollars a night each, plus eight bucks a beer. The place was basically full. Money was flowing in. But Jouvenal was a tightwad, a rare foreigner able to drive a hard bargain, and his Afghan waiters were seriously pissed off. "I am looking for something else," one young man in his twenties told me. "I hate it here." Was Jouvenal's attitude smart? Or was it provoking contempt?

Upon my return to the States I was amused to find a TripAdvisor review posted by one Steven1969. Steven wasn't satisfied with the facilities: "Large windows overlooking the courtyard were a risk from bomb blasts, even though they had some blast film on them."

EVERY NOW AND THEN, YOU SEE A REAL, LIVE PROFESSIONAL JOURNALIST.

CLICK

KAF

241

AS IT IS, TRAVELING INDEPENDENTLY BARELY LETS YOU SCRATCH THE SURFACE.

WHAT DO YOU THINK OF THE U.S.?

THE PROS ARE CREDENTIALED, SECURITIZED, AND INSULATED FROM REALITY.

CLICK

POLICE

WORST OF ALL, THEY LOOK RIDICULOUS.

Only non-soldier in miles wearing rented body armor

Permanent "Auntie Em, there's no place like home." Expression

TEDRALL

BETTER TO DIE. OR STAY HOME.

The Gandamack isn't marked by a street sign. You walk through an orange gate for the TNT express shipping service, which is across the street from the Iranian embassy, then farther away from the street. Like the entrances to medieval fortresses, getting into the Gandamack required us to pass through three sets of metal doors (each with barred peepholes) through a narrow corridor twisting around sharp corners. Once inside, you are supposedly allowed to keep a sidearm but are asked to check large automatic weapons at the sleepy front desk. (I never noticed any Glocks inside.) Aside from complimentary mosquito spray—an absolute necessity—the proprietors offer body armor to rent.

Security guards at the Gandamack Lodge, Kabul, formerly owned by Osama bin Laden

---

The streets of Kabul are lined with long, high blast walls topped with sandbags, concertina wire, and watchtowers manned by tricked-out young men brandishing, on the low end, AK-47s and RPGs, and, on the high end, antiaircraft guns loaded with armor-piercing shells.

There's an inverse relationship between local status and security. The more foreign an organization, not only in terms of the citizenship of its employees but also its culture, the higher the level of security precautions. American NGOs bristle with artillery. American outfits with a more populist touch, those that employ Afghans in positions with important titles, make do with a pair of skinny guards with AKs. Afghan stores that cater to Afghans have no security whatsoever.

It's the perfect allegory, not only for what went wrong for the United States in Afghanistan, but for the failure of foreign adventurism in general—primarily for the United States, but not exclusively. To put it in the jargon of modern and postmodern philosophy, the primordial fear of the Other is the driving force behind suppression and oppression. In Afghanistan, the United States is the Other. But it goes further than that: the United States invades Afghanistan, creates a bubble for itself within the Other, a Green Zone they call Bagram airbase (the irony of establishing itself in the same location used by the Soviets during their own failed occupation in the 1980s seemingly lost on them).

For the Americans in Afghanistan, the Afghans themselves are foreign, other, dangerous. Never mind that they're at home, living in their own country; indeed, they are not welcome anywhere else. In the final analysis, there is an excruciatingly simple reason that no country has successfully invaded and occupied another since the nineteenth century: they live there. We don't.

They have the home field advantage. In general that is enough to ensure victory. However, the U.S. refusal to go native, to live fearlessly in Afghanistan without blast walls or Kevlar or helmets or sunglasses, just hang out and walk around like an ordinary Afghan, the way Matt and Steven and I did (which Afghans and Americans alike deemed crazy and bizarre and yet here we are, back home all safe and sound), actually, to commit completely by importing our families and friends, intermarrying, starting businesses—that failure is why foreign adventurism doesn't stand a chance. We successfully occupy the former kingdom of Hawaii because we don't occupy it—we live there. We walk around, and we might get mugged or robbed—Oahu has one of the highest auto theft rates in the United States—but we are Americans and we feel and act as though we belong there.

You cannot occupy. You can only live. If no one kills you, congrats! You have earned the "right" to live there. But that's not the United States in Afghanistan (or Iraq or Haiti). We are afraid. Our fear defines us. As Osama bin Laden observed, we love life too much. And so our great war of civilizations against the people who live under the banner of Islam is doomed.

There was a movie theater around the corner from the Gandamack. It was playing a film called *AK-47*. We looked it up later online. It was a Bollywood production from 2008, concocted for the Afghan market. Film what you know, I guess. Our driver heard us talking about it. He got excited. "It is very, very good! Have you seen it?"

Kabul felt insulated. It was a city of fortresses, an armed camp. Atrocious air pollution, worse than the worst bad old days of Los Angeles in the 1970s, made our throats scratch and our eyes water. Anyway, it was full of NGO people and lame reporters. We hadn't come to see the same stuff as everyone else. We wanted to get out into the countryside to meet people who never got to talk to foreign journalists.

I was eager to get to Herat. North of Herat was the answer to a question I wanted answered and my second major self-assignment for Afghanistan 2010: Had construction begun on the Trans-Afghanistan oil and gas pipeline project? Major media reports said it had. But none of these were based on firsthand journalism. I wanted to know for certain. If so, it would mark the culmination of two decades of scheming on the part of U.S. and Afghan officials to exploit Afghanistan as a conduit for Central Asian energy resources. And if we didn't find anything, so be it.

Getting out of Kabul overland, however, was not easy. Especially if you wanted to go west.

The foreigners we talked to recommended that we call a company called Afghan Logistics. "They can get you anywhere in Afghanistan," a man who wouldn't tell us exactly what he did for a living told us. He had that dead giveaway Afrikaaner accent, though: merc. He was wrong. A few phone calls later, the manager called us. "Where do you want to go?" he wanted to know.

"The Central Route to Herat."

"I can take you as far as Charikar. Maybe Bamiyan." Bamiyan is the site of the Buddha statues blown up by the Taliban. It's maybe one-twentieth of the way to Herat.

"No, no, I need to cross the mountains. Through Ghor."

"Ghor?" There was a pause on the line. "Listen, my friend, take my advice. If you go that way, you are going to die. We have heard many bad reports from that road and that area."

"From where? Nothing I've seen says anything about central Afghanistan." Which was true. I'd been checking the Web for months. Nothing. Not that that meant much. After all, the reason we wanted to go that way was that no one ever went.

"No one will take you there. No amount of money will convince anyone to take you. If you go to Ghor, it is all Taliban. You will die. One hundred percent."

If I've learned anything, it's that nothing is a hundred percent. Okay, one thing was: he wasn't going to take me.

Soon we learned that neither would anyone else.

We went to taxi stands. Drivers gathered around, eager for the thousands of dollars we offered to make the journey. Once they understood exactly where we wanted to go, however, they drifted away, grumbling that we were crazy. We asked them where *they'd* be willing to go. The answer was basically nowhere. The airport. Just outside the Ring of Steel. No one was willing to venture far from the capital.

I called a military buddy stationed at Bagram airbase. "We're the only major employer in the country," he bragged. "I have some badass local drivers at my disposal. I'll find you a driver." He tried. No one wanted to go.

I worked my way through NGO contacts. I asked Afghan waiters

Panel 1:

I'M IN KABUL. STUCK, TRYING TO FIND A DRIVER TO TAKE US TO HERAT VIA THE CENTRAL HIGHWAY.

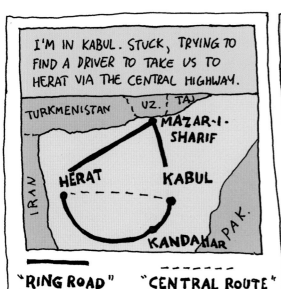

"RING ROAD" — "CENTRAL ROUTE"

Panel 2:

FEW KABULIS KNOW ABOUT THE CENTRAL ROUTE.

KANDAHAR IS TALIBAN EVERYWHERE!

IEDs!

TOO DAN-GEROUS!

NÉ... NO KANDAHAR. VIA BAMIYAN AND GHOR.

NO... NOT GHOR...

Panel 3:

GETTING THE RIGHT TEAM TOGETHER IS DIFFICULT.

WILLING DRIVER, BUT DRIVES SEDAN (NEED 4WD)

HAS A 4-RUNNER BUT DOESN'T KNOW THE WAY

KNOWS THE WAY BUT CAN'T DRIVE

I CAN GUIDE. AND I KNOW A DRIVER.*

*THIS GUY

UP FOR ANYTHING

[DARI? PASHTO? ???]

(CAN'T SPEAK ENGLISH AT ALL)

Panel 4:

SO WE SEARCH.

THAT WAS AFGHAN LOGISTICS. THE OUTFIT THAT CLAIMS TO BE 'UP FOR ANYTHING.'

LET ME GUESS. THEY'RE AFRAID TO GO THERE.

YUP.

AND WAIT.

Panel 5:

AND OUR MINDS TURN TO FUN, DANGEROUS THOUGHTS.

MOTOCYCLES

ONE WEEK AGO IN TALOQAN, THE HEAD OF THE LOCAL ENGLISH SCHOOL GAVE ME A CELLPHONE NUMBER FOR A JOVID WHO FIT THE DESCRIPTION OF "MY" JOVID, THE JOVID WHO GOT ME OUT OF AFGHANISTAN IN 2001 WHEN MURDERERS WERE COMING FOR ME. IS IT HIM? THERE'S ONLY ONE WAY TO FIND OUT.

EVERY FEW HOURS, I CALL THE NUMBER.

ALL I GET IS THREE RAPID BEEPS. HE IS OUT OF RANGE. OR HIS PHONE IS OFF.

I KEEP TRYING.

BEE-BEE-BEEP

IT'S $5 A MINUTE.

HOW MANY PEOPLE DID THIS DUDE LOSE?

BEE-BEE-BEEP

WHAT ELSE CAN I DO?

Call Failed

THE ROUTE TO WESTERN AFGHANISTAN HAVING BEEN CUT OFF IN THE NORTH AND THE SOUTH, OUR NEW PLAN IS TO TAKE THE MIDDLE WAY. THE CENTRAL ROUTE TAKES YOU THROUGH THE MOST RUGGED AND REMOTE AREAS IN A MOST RUGGED AND REMOTE COUNTRY — MOST NOTABLY, THE MUCH-STORIED

PROVINCE OF GHOR.

MINARET OF JAM
SHAHBAL DISTRICT

GHOR IS ETHNICALLY DIVERSE: TAJIK, HAZARA, UZBEK, AND A FEW PASHTUNS. IT IS A PLACE FEW AFGHANS GET TO SEE.

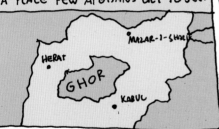

HERAT

MAZAR-I-SHARIF

GHOR

KABUL

IT BECAME FAMOUS BECAUSE OF JOSIAH HARLAN, THE FIRST AMERICAN IN AFGHANISTAN. HARLAN WAS A QUAKER, AN ADVENTURER, AND A CHARMER WHO USED HIGH-TECH U.S. WEAPONS TO IMPRESS MOHAMMED REFFEE BEG HAZARA.

Inspired Rudyard Kipling's story "The Man Who Would Be King"

IN 1838, HAZARA APPOINTED HARLAN AND HIS HEIRS, IN PERPETUITY, PRINCE OF GHOR IN EXCHANGE FOR MILITARY SUPPORT. BUT THEN THE BRITS INVADED IN 1839 AND KICKED HIM OUT.

WEIRD STORY.

NOW HARLAN'S HEIR AS PRINCE OF GHOR IS SCOTT REINIGER, AN ACTOR FROM "DAWN OF THE DEAD."

IF FLOODS AND CORRUPT COPS AND LOUSY ROADS AND TALIBS AND BANDITS ALLOW — INSHALLAH — WE SHALL SEE GHOR IN THE NEXT WEEK.

$250 A DAY PLUS GAS? WE'RE NOT MADE OF MONEY!

HT

for help. Here we were with thousands of dollars burning a hole in the pockets of our *shalwar kameezes* in the world's poorest nation, yet nobody wanted to take them.

If those recalcitrant cabbies saved our lives—which is obviously possible, maybe even probable—then: thanks.

We were stuck in Kabul five days.

They were not without note.

Down Chari Sadarat from the Gandamack is the Shah Mohammed Bookstore, made famous (or, depending on your point of view, infamous) by *The Bookseller of Kabul* by Asne Seierstad. The Shah M offers the most comprehensive collection of works in English and other European languages about Afghanistan, Pakistan, India, and Central Asia that I've ever seen. Prices are steep, reflecting the costs of owner Mohammed Rais's numerous buying trips. I picked up *Afghanistan: From Darius to Amunullah*, a 1979 reprint of a 1934 history by British Lieutenant General George F. MacMunn, for thirty-two dollars. Sadly, the MacMunn title I really wanted, *Black Velvet: A Drama of India and the Bomb Cult* (also 1934), was not on offer.

Matt, Steven, and I were barely in the store five minutes when Rais stood up from behind the counter and asked: "Are you Ted Rall? I have sold two hundred forty copies of your book." He pulled a copy of *To Afghanistan and Back* off the shelf. "Forty dollars each!" I was so happy to be recognized, especially at this odd corner of the globe, that I didn't complain about the failure of my royalty statements to reflect his windfall profit. If only I had sales like that in the States . . .

Also, Matt got sick. It was evening. Steven and I were sitting at a table in the courtyard of the Gandamack, unwinding after another day of driving around Kabul in search of a driver willing to take us to Herat. The woman from Al Jazeera casually walked up to us and informed us, almost offhandedly: "Your friend is ill or something." We found Matt sitting on the side of his bed, rubbing his head. His skin

Fortress Kabul: Hamid Karzai's "Ring of Steel"

Store owned by Shah Mohammed Rais, the "Bookseller of Kabul." He recognized me at once.

was gray. He had been in the bathroom. He had passed out, probably from not eating enough, and banged his head against the sink. The food at the Gandamack, though far short of execrable, was less than enticing.

He slept hard and long that night. He was pretty much fine the next day. Not bad for a first-time international traveler.

Afghanistan defeated the British and the Russians. Us too.

No one was going to drive us to Herat. The closest we got to a ride was a guy who showed up with a Toyota 4Runner filled with jerry cans and cases of water. We negotiated a cutthroat rate—more than five hundred dollars a day—for only a partial journey. He offered to take us to Chaghcheran, provincial capital of Ghor province in the center of the country, where he claimed we would be able to hitch a ride the rest of the way from a passing truck driver. (When we did go to Chaghcheran, by the way, this turned out to be untrue. There was no through traffic whatsoever.) We told him to come by the next morning.

An hour later he called to say he wanted out. "It's a lot of money," he allowed. "But I will not be able to spend it. I will either be killed by the Taliban or by robbers, or the Afghan police will steal it."

I was furious. "Fuck it," I told Matt and Steven, sitting at our all-too-familiar table at the Gandamack Lodge. "We'll take the fucking plane."

Kabul airport was small and ramshackle, with many signs bearing pictures of AK-47s with an X through them. To deter truck and car bombs we were made to walk several hundred yards from the taxi dropoff point through a series of narrow defiles, desultorily patted down by soldiers who would have missed grenades had we been carrying them. We put our stuff up for the X-ray machine and pushed it through because the conveyor belt wasn't running. Which made sense because, as I noticed when we were waved through, the whole machine wasn't on.

Afghanistan has adapted to modern air travel; the waiting areas were sterile, depressing, and uncomfortable. Plastic chairs, sealed windows, not enough ventilation. The tarmac was a parade of U.N. planes

Nazary Four Star Hotel, Herat

of all shapes and sizes. I snapped a photo, and an Afghan soldier tapped me on the shoulder and threatened to confiscate my camera. Just like home.

As the plane corkscrewed through the smog, the mostly male passengers burst into smiles. Ramadan! There's an exception for travelers. Not food, but water bottles rolled down the aisle on a cart. I looked down at Kabul, thinking to myself, what a remarkably ugly city.

IN 2001 I MET A COLLEAGUE, A FELLOW WAR CORRESPONDENT, WHO HAD HIRED AN AFGHAN DRIVER TO TAKE HIM THROUGH THE KHYBER PASS.

WE GOT AMBUSHED JUST A FEW MILES PAST THE BORDER.

"AS HE ACCELERATED INTO 2 GUNMEN BLOCKING OUR WAY, THEY OPENED FIRE."

"HE LIVED LONG ENOUGH TO GET ME OVER A RIDGE, OUT OF RANGE."

I SAID YOU'D BE SAFE. YOU'RE SAFE... NOW...

WHATEVER HAPPENED TO THOSE COURAGEOUS AFGHANS?

WILL YOU TAKE ME TO THE FRONT?

WHY NOT?*

* STANDARD AFGHAN REPLY

IN '01 NO ONE HESITATED TO DRIVE ME THROUGH BATTLES. NOW YOU CAN'T GET A DRIVER THROUGH A SKETCHY AREA.

SEE YOU AT 7 AM!

Called 10 minutes later to weasel out

MATT, STEVEN, AND I SPENT 5 DAYS LOOKING FOR DRIVERS FROM KABUL TO HERAT. NO ONE WOULD GO. NOT EVEN FOR $500 A DAY.

$200 A DAY.
OK
$300
OK

AFGHANS AND FOREIGNERS ALIKE AGREE ON THE EXPLANATION.

IN '01 PEOPLE WERE OPTIMISTS. BUT 9 YEARS OF U.S. IMPOTENCE HAS DEMORALIZED THEM MORE THAN 23 YEARS OF CIVIL WAR. IF THE U.S. CAN'T HELP AFGHANISTAN, NO ONE CAN.

FINALLY, WE FLEW TO HERAT.

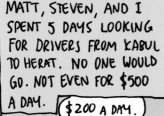

SPIRALING OUT OF KABUL TO

AVOID MISSILES

EVEN THE PILOTS ARE COWARDS.

ONE MONTH EACH YEAR, DEVOUT MUSLIMS GO WITHOUT FOOD OR WATER FROM DAWN TO DUSK.

Lots of napping and random taking it easy

THERE ARE CONSEQUENCES.

FASTING IS ESPECIALLY DIFFICULT IN DRY AND DUSTY AND HOT AFGHANISTAN. AND THIS YEAR, IT'S EVEN WORSE BECAUSE RAMADAN FALLS IN AUGUST.

WHAT DO YOU **WANT?!**

Cranky

Armed

DAYS ARE LOOONNG. AND REALLY HOT.

BY MID-AFTERNOON, MANY AFGHANS ARE A WRECK.

WH-? DID YOU SAY SOMETHING? I'M SORRY...HUH? I DON'T.

MOTORCYCLES AND CARS WEAVE DANGEROUSLY ACROSS TRAFFIC.

STUDIES OF ISLAMIC COUNTRIES SHOW THEY LOSE 1/12 TH OF ANNUAL PRODUCTIVITY DUE TO RAMADAN.

THERE'S A LITTLE WIGGLE ROOM. YOU CAN RINSE YOUR MOUTH (AND SPIT OUT THE WATER). YOU CAN SUCK ON A WET CLOTH. KIDS ARE EXEMPT, AS ARE THE ELDERLY AND INFIRM. AND TRAVELERS.

SPLOOSH

Mouth "Accidentally" Open

A LOT OF PEOPLE CHEAT. A LOT.

THE BEVERAGE SERVICE ON PAMIR AIR FROM KABUL TO HERAT WAS WATER ONLY, BUT IT WAS GREETED AS THOUGH IT WERE ICE-COLD BEER.

FLY WITH PRINCE

HERAT

YOU'VE SEEN THE PIPELINE FROM TURK-MENISTAN?

YES. IT IS 120 KM. NORTH OF HERAT.

THE HIGHWAY NORTH TO THE TURKMEN BORDER IS BLEAK.

DON'T SAY I NEVER TAKE YOU GUYS ANYWHERE.

FINALLY, WE ARRIVE AT THE BORDER. STILL NO PIPELINE.

IF IT — ACTUAL CONSTRUCTION — EXISTED, WE WOULD HAVE SEEN IT ON THIS STRETCH OF HIGHWAY. THE TRANS-AFGHANISTAN PIPELINE EXISTS... BUT ONLY ON PAPER.

THAT MAN SAYS THERE WAS AN OIL PIPELINE FROM TURKMENISTAN — BUT PEOPLE TOOK IT TO BUILD A MOSQUE.

SOON

THERE IT IS!

THOSE PIPES ARE A FOOT THICK. WATER PIPES. SEWAGE, MAYBE.

NO! THEY BROUGHT OIL DURING SOVIET TIMES!

LET'S GO.

JUST TWO WEEKS AGO, PRESIDENT KARZAI ANNOUNCED HIS DESIRE TO RESUME CONSTRUCTION ON THE T.A.P. PIPELINE. AT THIS RATE, HOWEVER, THERE WON'T EVER BE ENOUGH PIPE TO LOOT FOR A MINI-MOSQUE.

THIS IS LIKE THE "STONEHENGE" SCENE IN "SPINAL TAP."

1 FOOT
Our Lady of the Stolen Soviet Sewage Pipe

A VISIT TO THE FRIDAY MOSQUE, HERAT, NORTHWESTERN AFGHANISTAN

EXCUSE ME... WHERE ARE YOU FROM? WHAT ARE YOU DOING HERE?

AMERICA. WE ARE JOURNALISTS.

A LONG CONVERSATION FOLLOWED.

WHAT SHOULD THE U.S. DO?

WE DON'T NEED SOLDIERS. WHY CAN'T YOU SEND **HELP**?

LOTS OF AFGHANS JOINED THE DIALOGUE.

WHEN AMERICA CAME AFTER 11 SEPTEMBER, WE THOUGHT: "GOOD! YOU WILL HELP US BUILD OUR COUNTRY!"

BUT NOW IT SEEMS LIKE AMERICA JUST WANTS TO TAKE FROM AFGHANISTAN.

IT WAS GETTING DARK, SO...

PEOPLE ARE INCREDIBLY NICE TO US.

IT'S AMAZING. ESPECIALLY WHEN YOU CONSIDER THAT OUR COUNTRY HAS BRUTALIZED, HUMILIATED, AND SUBJUGATED THEM.

@#★!!!

SIX: COMING APRIL 2067: THE TRANS-AFGHANISTAN PIPELINE

About 735 kilometers of the [Trans-Afghanistan] pipeline will pass through Afghanistan, including the violent Kandahar province that has high Taliban presence, and 800 kilometers will pass through Pakistan, including its tribal areas, posing a big security challenge to the project.

—*The Wall Street Journal*, January 2011

My second major self-assignment in Afghanistan was to determine the status of the Trans-Afghanistan oil and gas pipeline. Various reports in the international press had claimed that construction had already begun along the highway north of Herat near the Turkmen border. Was that true? There was only one way to find out.

Though still in a war zone and clearly subject to the same dangers as the rest of the country, Herat felt relatively low-key. The city is relatively flush with cash thanks to its proximity to international border crossings with Iran and Turkmenistan, and it has benefited from its long control by Ishmael Khan, an ethnic Tajik warlord who expropriated toll collections from trucks transporting goods but used most of the funds to build infrastructure and create public welfare programs.

We checked into the Nazary Four Star Hotel on Walatay Street in the Cinema district. Disappointment number one: the Nazary is two stars at best, and that's by Afghan standards. Disappointment two: the

movie theater had been destroyed years earlier by the Taliban. The owner was helpful, however, and arranged for a driver to meet us the next morning.

"He says he has seen your pipeline," the Nazary's owner assured me as we all shook hands. "He has seen where it is being built. It is north of here, near Turkmenistan."

That was exactly what I wanted to hear.

Afghans are good at telling you exactly what you want to hear.

STILL A DREAM
PRESIDENTS AND BANKERS, BUT NO ACTION ON THE GROUND
SEPTEMBER 21, 2010

Kara-Tepe, Afghanistan—There is no pipeline. There probably won't be one. Yet the pipeline-that-will-never-exist is one of the main reasons that hundreds of thousands of Afghans and two thousand American soldiers are dead.

Also known as Turkmenistan-Afghanistan-Pakistan, the Trans-Afghanistan Pipeline (TAP) would carry the world's biggest new energy reserves, which are in Kazakhstan and Turkmenistan's sections of the landlocked Caspian Sea, across Afghanistan to a deep-sea port in Pakistan. (A modified version of the plan, TAPI, would add an extension to India.)

Some background:

The idea dates to the mid-1990s. Unocal, owner of the Union 76 gas station chain, led a consortium of oil companies that negotiated with the Taliban government. Among their consultants was Zalmay Khalilzad, who later served as Bush's ambassador to Afghanistan, Iraq, and the United Nations. (While in Kabul, Khalilzad engineered the U.S.-backed coup that installed Hamid Karzai—also a former Unocal consultant—over the wishes of the loya jirga.*)

As you'd expect, political instability has been the primary obstacle preventing a "New Silk Road" of oil and gas to flow across Central and South Asia. The planned route for TAP follows Afghanistan's "ring road" from the northwestern city of Herat across soaring mountains and bleak deserts through Kandahar province, the heart of Taliban territory. Hundreds of warlords and regional commanders would have to be paid protection money.

Unocal pulled out in 1998, citing the civil war between the Taliban and the Northern Alliance. But logic can't kill a dream.

In February 2001 the new Bush-Cheney administration invited Taliban representatives to Texas for new talks. When the Afghans insisted upon higher transit fees than the White House oilmen were prepared to offer, things turned ugly. "Either you accept our offer of a carpet of gold," a frustrated U.S. negotiator snapped at the Talibs on May 15, 2001, "or we bury you under a carpet of bombs."

The last Bush-Taliban pipeline discussions took place on August 2, 2001, in Islamabad between Assistant Secretary of State Christina Rocca, a former CIA employee, and Abdul Salam Zaeef, the Taliban ambassador to Pakistan. (By the way, Zaeef's memoir, *My Life in the Taliban*, is riveting.)

The 9/11 attacks, planned in Pakistan and carried out by Pakistani-trained Saudis and Egyptians, provided the pretext for invading Afghanistan. Was TAP the only motivation? Certainly not: Afghanistan also offered a "dry run" invasion of a defenseless Muslim nation

---

* A loya jirga is a "grand assembly," analogous to a constitutional convention or ad hoc Congress in the West. Tribal leaders and high-profile Afghans convene to discuss and debate major issues such as a constitution, as well as political issues or national emergencies. It may also be used for resolving disputes.

pre-Iraq, as well as a chance to exert geopolitical muscle flexing at the expense of regional rivals Russia and Iran. But TAP was part of the calculus.

Since 2002 the presidents of Turkmenistan, Pakistan, and Afghanistan have repeatedly met to talk about TAP(I). The Asian Development Bank has financed feasibility studies for the $8 billion deal.

"Of late, Turkmen President Gurbanguly Berdymukhammedov has spoken often of TAPI," U.S. government–backed Radio Free Europe / Radio Liberty reported on September 14, 2010. "He has contacted the leaders of Afghanistan, Pakistan, and India since the start of September to arrange meetings in New York and Ashkhabat. Berdymukhammedov is calling for a summit of TAPI leaders in Ashkhabat in December."

Politicians want the pipeline. Bankers want it too. But has ground been broken? A number of mainstream news accounts said yes, that the 52-inch pipe was already being laid along the highway that runs north from Herat to the Turkmen border.

I wanted confirmation. And photos. Something to shove in the faces of those neocons who dismiss TAP as a conspiracy theory made up out of whole cloth. "If petroleum—the mineral most favored by the Bush administration—were the primary motivation for stationing NATO soldiers in Afghanistan, then why would President Bush have diverted a majority of the resources necessary to secure the country (including soldiers, supplies, and money) so early in the game to Iraq?" asked one. Um, because Iraq has more?

Unfortunately, all the journalists in Afghanistan are embedded with soldiers, running around the mountains near the Pakistani border in a war that is irrelevant to the Afghan people but looks good on the nightly news. They're too busy supporting the troops to do any real reporting. So, accompanied by fellow cartoonists Matt Bors and Steven Cloud, I set out up that road from Herat two weeks ago.

My goal: the Trans-Afghanistan Pipeline. Not on paper. In real life.

It's a hot, dusty drive. There isn't much to see: desert, scrub, goatherds, adobe-style mudbrick villages. The Koshk District, the region's major population center, is so infested with Talibs that Afghan national policemen are afraid to drive through. I can tell you what you don't see: the Trans-Afghanistan Pipeline. There's no construction of any kind alongside that highway.

There was, however, fun to be had.

We stopped locals to ask them about TAP. Finally, one geezer brightened up. He had seen it! Our Afghan driver got excited. He turned to us: "It was here! But the local people stole it."

"They stole the Trans-Afghanistan Pipeline?"

"Yes! They used it to make a mosque. He is going to show us."

I was happy. What a story! I took out my camera, ready to document the amazing tale of the Our Lady of TAP mosque, indirectly financed by American hubris. We followed the man down an alley and across a small garden. He walked us into what can only be described as a modest building. Less charitably, as a dump.

I am not charitable.

He gestured. *There it is!* said his gesture. There, indeed it was: a dumpy little building, which I'll call a mosque though there was no way to identify it as a house of god, with pipes holding up the corners and serving as rafters. Small pipes. Very small pipes.

Nine-inch pipes. Maybe eight.

"That's not an oil pipeline," I told my driver. "What we're looking for is big. I made a big circle with my arms. "*Biiigg.*"

He pointed again. He smiled as if to say: Look harder.

"This pipeline came from Turkmenistan," said my driver. "I was a boy when the Soviets built it. For oil."

North toward Turkmenistan from Herat, in search of the Trans-Afghanistan Pipeline

"No. This is a water pipe," I said. "Or maybe sewage. Besides, we're looking for something new. Not Soviet."

Because it seemed rude not to, I snapped a few photos and tipped the old guy. It was like that scene in *Spinal Tap* when the mini-Stonehenge drops from the ceiling. I stifled a laugh as we got back into our car.

SEVEN: SLEEPING WITH THE TALIBAN

Afghans (including the Taliban) are not anti-American.
—Robert Young Pelton, author of
The World's Most Dangerous Places

Feudalism, if it ever left, has returned to Afghanistan. During the Middle Ages, government, such as it was, existed within fortified city walls. Between the cities were vast forests, robbers, wolves—anarchy. Civilized people left the confines of their reinforced walls as infrequently as possible, and then only in quick dashes to other cities.

So it is today in Afghanistan. The central government, such as it is, controls a few big cities: Kabul and, to a lesser extent, Mazar-i-Sharif, Herat, and, nominally, Kandahar. The rest—the farms, small towns and villages, opium fields, robbers, and whatever wild animals have managed to avoid getting killed and eaten—belong to the Taliban. Sayed Muhammad Gulabzoi, an Afghan parliamentarian who served as interior minister in the Soviet-backed Afghan government during the 1980s, says the bad old days are back: "In those days, the provincial capitals were in the hands of the government, while the *mujahideen* controlled the villages. We see the same thing happening with the Taliban and the government today."

Urban Afghans would rather face wolves than the neo-Taliban. Or, for that matter, the corrupt Afghan policemen and soldiers who ring

Shortly before being detained by Afghan troops and police in Taliban-held Do Ab, Herat province

the cities to shake them down. Which is why it was impossible to get anyone to drive us out of Kabul. To Kabulis, Afghanistan outside of Kabul had might as well not exist. It is terra incognita . . . terror incognito. They may not be able to wish it away. As they are well aware, the hinterlands can and will come to them at any moment, as it did during the mid-nineties. But they sure as hell aren't going there voluntarily.

It was the same in Herat. My third goal had been to cover the interior of the country, where Western journalists never ventured. The latest edition of the Lonely Planet guide to Afghanistan reflected this; there was literally no coverage whatsoever of the country's western desert along the border with Iran.

But there were no buses. Nor were there drivers willing to go there.

"You should not go by car," the Nazary's owner counseled me. "It is better to fly." I was sick and tired of this advice. So many people had told me the same thing in Kabul, I had stopped counting. "We need to

FEW INSTITUTIONS IN THE U.S.-OCCUPIED "NEW AFGHANISTAN" DRAW AS MUCH SCORN AS THE AFGHAN NATIONAL POLICE. UNDERPAID AND HIGHLY ENDANGERED— THE TALIBAN KILL 5 TO 10 OF THEM A DAY, INCLUDING BY METHODS LIKE POISONING THEIR FOOD—THEIR RANKS ATTRACT THE DIMWITTED AND DESPERATE. THEY ARE WIDELY VIEWED AS CORRUPT, COWARDLY, AND USELESS.

NOT NOW, IN FRONT OF YOUR FOREIGN PASSENGERS. BUT YOU HAVE TO COME BACK THIS WAY, GIVE ME 3,000 AFGHANIS* THEN.

* ~US$60

CHECKPOINT, MAZAR-I-SHARIF TO KABUL

THEIR **RIDICULOUS UNIFORMS** CERTAINLY DON'T BUILD ESPRIT DE CORPS.

GRAY-BLUE, JUST LIKE THE CUSTODIAN'S OUTFIT IT RESEMBLES

OVERALL DESIGN: LIKE THE DHARMA INITIATIVE UNIFORMS IN "LOST"

PATCH DESIGNED BY COMMITTEE

FRENCH KÉPIS LOOK CUTE. THIS HAT LOOKS OAFISH

RANDOM BUCKLES (I EVEN SAW SOVIET!)

POCKETS AHOY! MEMBERS ONLY, LOOK OUT

NO GUN, MOSTLY

IT'S ALMOST LIKE THE AMERICANS WHO PICKED THESE UNIFORMS WANTED AFGHAN COPS TO FEEL LIKE CHUMPS.

AFGHAN COPS IN ACTION!

Texting

DIRECTING TRAFFIC

Z

FIGHTING INSURGENTS

STOP

REVENUE RAISING

talk to Afghans outside of the cities," I kept insisting. "Americans need to know what all Afghans think about things, not just those who live in the big cities."

THE DEATH OF HOPE
IF THE UNITED STATES CAN'T HELP AFGHANISTAN, WHO CAN?
SEPTEMBER 1, 2010

Do Ab, Afghanistan—Afghanistan has more infrastructure than it did in 2001. But Afghans also have less soul.

In many ways, Afghanistan was a more dangerous country nine years ago. There were more mines, more random acts of violence, warlordism everywhere. U.S. warplanes were bombing everything that moved. But, particularly in the Tajik-dominated north, there was also boundless optimism, a feeling that anything was possible. Good times might not be right around the corner—not exactly. But soon.

If anyone could fix Afghanistan, people thought, the United States could. The superpower colossus! A nation so rich that Afghans couldn't begin to measure, much less really understand it. Rebuilding Afghanistan from the ground up would be chump change for mighty America.

The U.S. media did nothing to temper Afghan optimism. An October 2001 piece for *Slate* was typical: "Terrorism, the most ardent proponents of intervention argue, can't be defeated without a complete reconstruction of Afghanistan's government, infrastructure and society," wrote Damien Cave. "In effect, what is needed is a 21st century version of the Marshall Plan that rebuilt Europe after World War II." (Cave's piece now reads like Cassandra. If only we'd followed the advice of a certain Joe Biden back then.) Nation building? We were all for it. Everyone—especially right-wing media types—promoted the "Marshall Plan for Afghanistan" meme.

Back then, Afghans were brave. When I needed a driver to take me to the front—the front! where bombs were falling by the thousands! where the Taliban were shooting at us from a hundred yards away!—I'd have a dozen guys vying for the job.

Now, alas, Afghans are utterly demoralized. The Taliban, in bands of forty to four hundred each, terrorize whole provinces. No one—not even the cops—dare travel outside the major cities. Where the suburbs begin, so does fear. Whenever I go somewhere, Afghan officials ask me: Where are my bodyguards? Where is my body armor? Why am I outside Kabul? "If you were a real journalist," a police official told me, typically, "you'd be traveling in a truck full of U.S. soldiers with big guns." (Funny me, I thought it was the other way around.)

The Afghans, those badass Afghans, are afraid. I looked for drivers everywhere—at taxi stands, through personal contacts, the U.N., even the military. No one would take me outside a city. Price didn't matter. In a country where a civil servant earns thirty dollars a month, I offered drivers five hundred dollars a day—and got turned down. "It's just too dangerous," people kept saying—too dangerous to be seen with foreigners, and too dangerous without them too. (Messing with Westerners can cause trouble. In Afghanistan in 2010, everything causes trouble.)

Even allowing for the risk of Taliban attacks, Afghan highways are safer than they were in 2001. Thanks to paved roads, you can go faster and evade ambushes if need be. There are government gun nests every few kilometers. Unlike '01, you don't have American jets bombing everything that moves on Afghan highways. Yet Afghans are far less willing to take chances now than they were then. What happened?

The Afghan sense of what is possible has narrowed. When it came to bombs and high-tech gadgets for killing Afghans, the United States spent like there was no tomorrow. Meanwhile, the construction budget was less than one-half of one percent. Of which most was never spent. And what actually did get spent got stolen. For a while, Afghans concocted elaborate conspiracy theories to explain this insane set of misplaced priorities. They couldn't believe that America the Superpower was so stupid, incompetent, and/or corrupt.

They believe it now. And the effect has been devastating. "If America, with its unchallenged military power and massive material wealth, cannot or will not help Afghanistan," a college student named Mohammed told me at the Friday Mosque in Herat, "who can? If they can't build houses, who can? Why can't they catch the Taliban?"

I have been hearing this a lot: from NGO workers who have been here for years, Western journalists, and Afghan citizens. We were Afghanistan's last hope, and we blew it.

Now that political support for the war is waning in the United States, the Obama administration is looking to start pulling out next year. Actually, that isn't adding to Afghans' sense of hopelessness. They gave up on the United States years ago. Even if we were to stick around, people here say, they don't believe that we'd suddenly start helping ordinary Afghans or lift a finger to provide basic security.

They're screwed and they know it.

Killing Afghans' hope for a better future may be an even more vile crime than the hundreds of thousands of Afghans the United States has murdered with bombs and bullets. As the United States stands by and watches, the security and economic situations continue to deteriorate. So Afghan psychology is reverting to survival skills learned during the Soviet occupation, civil war, and Taliban period. People are keeping their heads down, not taking chances.

Without optimism, after all, courage is illogical.

By most accounts Zabol is the kind of place where you can open fire with an automatic weapon with no danger of hitting an honest man. Known for its "one hundred twenty day wind" dust storm, this trading town in southeastern Iran is reputed to be the nation's biggest security problem: full of wild-eyed Afghan drug and gun runners. This was to be our entry point to Iran and our exit from Afghanistan. We would drive south from Herat down the A1 highway, hang a right at Zaranj, and get picked up by an Iranian fixer at the Kang border crossing. It sounded grim and strange and right up my alley.

It was not to be.

When in Rome and all that, so we adapted to the reality of the New Afghanistan by hopping another Pamir Air flight, this one to Chaghcheran, the tiny provincial capital of rural Ghor province. About fifteen thousand Aimaq, Hazaras, and Tajiks lived there. We'd get to see the Afghan interior after all. But we'd have to hopscotch over the Taliban—who held all of Afghanistan except its major cities—to get there.

On the flight to Chaghcheran a young man, a seventeen-year-old high school student, insisted that for journalists there was only one place to stay in town: the PRT near the airport. Lonely Planet said there were *chaikhanas* (teahouses) where foreigners could bed down for a nominal fee, but those had apparently been shut down since the time of that writing due to the deteriorating security situation. Now the only option was the Provincial Reconstruction Team, a military base run by Lithuania under the auspices of the International Security Assistance Force, also known as the U.S. occupation authorities. This, according to our new friend, was the only place where journalists were allowed to stay in Ghor province.

The plane touched down on a dusty landing strip on a blazing hot day. At the end of the runway was a gutted plane of mysterious military vintage; we couldn't tell if it had crashed or merely been abandoned

I COULDN'T BELIEVE IT.

THE NATO BASE AT CHAGHCHERAN THREW US OUT FOR LACK OF ISAF ACCREDITATION — IN THE MIDDLE OF THE NIGHT.

NO ONE GOES OUT AT NIGHT IN AFGHANISTAN.

IT WAS MY OWN FAULT. I **NEVER** COOPERATE WITH OFFICIALDOM. THEY **ALWAYS** SCREW YOU OVER.

THIS WAS EXACTLY WHAT I'D BEEN OBSESSIVELY AVOIDING: A MILITARY ESCORT, SOLDIERS BRISTLING WITH HIGH-POWERED WEAPONRY, ATTRACTING ATTENTION LIKE GANGBUSTERS.

GREAT... WE'RE TOTALLY GONNA GET IED'D

Gunner

PLEASE TO GIVE OUR FRIENDS A GOOD ROOM.

I WANT TO DIE

Lobb

VERY BAD NEWS: EVERYONE IN TOWN KNOWS WHERE WE'RE STAYING — AND THAT IT'S A PLACE WITH NO SECURITY WHATSOEVER.

WHOA — WHAT'S THAT **SMELL**?! HOSPITAL MOP...

SLIGHTLY LESS BAD: WE WERE BACK TO AUTHENTICITY.

THEY'RE **SINGING**! AT 2 AM! WHAT ARE THEY **DOING**?!

@✶#! RAMADAN...

@#✶ SMELL...

PAMIR HOTEL, CHAGHCHERAN

there. We grabbed our bags and trudged in the heat about a mile down the road to the entrance of the PRT.

The guards made us wait about half an hour. They were the first soldiers we'd talked to; we'd caught glimpses of Kevlar-covered troops riding transports in Mazar and Kabul. Finally a Lithuanian press attaché, thrilled that he finally had something to do—"No journalists ever come here," he complained—told us we could stay. We filed into the base, were led into a sterile briefing room, and sat through a quick rundown of dos and don'ts. Next he gave us keys to our rooms.

We were in a barracks full of soldiers from various NATO countries, mostly former Soviet republics like Latvia and Belarus. There was a cot, a rough military blanket, a sad pillow, and about half of one bar on wifi. It was like a dorm, albeit the crappiest dorm ever. My room had obviously been previously assigned to some American special forces soldier: there were New York Yankees stickers and a "9/11—Never Forget" yellow ribbon decal on the walls. By Afghan standards, and for Ghor province, it was the height of luxury: electricity, air-conditioning, and half a bar of wifi.

We were there four hours.

They threw us out. We were scared, with good reason.

"Can you drop us around the corner?" The last thing we needed was to show up late at night, during fast-breaking time at Ramadan, accompanied by heavily armed soldiers in a convoy of APCs and Humvees. They ignored me.

We pulled up in front of what turned out to be the only place in town that would put up foreigners, the Pamir Hotel. The door wasn't closed. There was no door.

We entered the shoddy, still unfinished four-story building and climbed up to the third floor. An old Afghan man with a magnificent white beard greeted us and showed us to our room. "You are our guests," he said happily, "and we will make you happy here." This was going to be a challenge. We walked down a long corridor. It was a full house. All the doors were open. Inside seated on the ground breaking fast were a bunch of fierce Afghan men. They glared. We smiled. They glared harder.

We were in a hotel full of Talibs.

The first thing I noticed about our room was the stench. The second was the dark red stain on the carpet. The third and fourth were the bullet holes—one in the window, the other in the wall about five feet above the stain. Great. Someone had bought it in our room. Otherwise it was standard issue: red carpet in the middle, grotty mats lining the walls, broken windows to let in the flies and plague-bearing mosquitoes.

"Got any rooms in the inside?" I asked. "Away from the window?"

No answer. But I knew the answer. The place was full. Better not to make a fuss.

There was no other place in town willing to house foreigners. The roads to Bamiyan and Herat were considered impassable due to insurgent attacks; therefore no one bothered to try to pass them. The next flight out was Sunday. For better or worse, the Pamir Hotel would be our home for the next four nights.

Matt and Steven struck up a conversation with a pair of Afghans across the hall. One looked to be about sixty, the other twenty-five. The older one did most of the talking.

"They've invited us to break fast with them," Steven said. I sat down.

"During the Soviet war," the older man said, "I operated a Stinger missile. I shot down Russian helicopters. It was a great time in my life." It was obviously not the first time he had told this story. Now he was a member of Hezb-i-Islami, a group founded by Gulbuddin Hekmatyar that was officially designated a terrorist organization by the U.S. State Department after Hekmatyar had the temerity to oppose Karzai and to escape a 2002 assassination attempt by the CIA. To keep things interesting, our dining companion was also a water expert

DAY 3: GHOR PROVINCE. THE DAYS ARE BORING, HOT AND DUSTY. THE NIGHTS ARE CREEPY.

French doors to ledge, easy walk to our front window

Our room

Skeevy Taliban types, playing cards

OUR 4TH FLOOR HALLWAY

IT'S RAMADAN, SO MOTORCYCLES ROAR UP AT ANY AND ALL HOURS.

THE **TALIBAN** DRIVE MOTORCYCLES... (BUT SO DOES EVERYONE ELSE)

VRRROOM

OUR AFGHAN HOTEL NEIGHBORS START PARTYING AT 2 AM EVERY NIGHT.

Afghans like to slam doors

HA HA SLAM!

ONE DUDE CONSTANTLY HACKS UP PHLEGM.

CRAKGHSHR SCHRAAAK

I WISH HE'D JUST DIE ALREADY.

THE CREEPY PART IS THAT THERE'S NO SECURITY WHATSOEVER.

Our hotel entrance. No guard. No Door.

IF TALIBS CAME FOR US, THEY'D JUST WALK IN. NO ONE WOULD LIFT A FINGER TO PROTECT US.

WITH LUCK, THAT WON'T HAPPEN. OR, AS AFGHANS SAY, INSHALLAH — IF GOD WILLS IT.

SLAM!

@*#!

FEAR DOESN'T MAKE YOU ANY SAFER.

employed by the Afghan government to work on irrigation and potable water schemes for Ghor province.

The young man piped in. "You are *Americans*?" We affirmed this.

"America is big boss country, yes?"

We didn't know what to say.

He went on. "America likes to tell other countries what to do, yes? America thinks it's funny to kill Afghans, yes? Killing women and children, even at their weddings, yes?"

"No, no, no," I said, waving my hands. This is not good. "Not at all. The American government, yes, they are assholes," I said. "But the American people are mostly not like that. Most Americans are against the war here." Which was true. At the time. The polls had turned against the war. But not everywhere. In the South, in the rural areas—rural areas like the one we were in—Americans still thought invading countries full of hardened Muslim fighters was a fantastic idea. I didn't think it necessary to explain the details.

He grinned. "Relax, my friend. How do you say—I am just fucking with you, man."

We had a long, nervous laugh.

He took a different tack.

"What are you doing here?" he asked. "You are with the military? We saw you arrive with the soldiers."

We told him the truth, that the NATO guys had thrown us out in the middle of the night, that they only worked with reporters unworthy of the name, men and women who toed the official line. "Here we are," I said. Which was undeniable.

"You must be very brave," he said, "to come here."

"Why?" I asked. "Are you going to hurt us?"

Nervous laughter, this time tilted more toward the Afghan side of the room. Two more men had sat down. They sized us up.

"Nooo," he said.

ISLAM REQUIRES A HUSBAND TO PROVIDE EVERYTHING TO HIS WIFE THAT SHE NEEDS AT HOME. THAT WAY SHE NEVER NEEDS TO GO OUT.

OF COURSE SOMETIMES SHE MUST GO OUT FOR SOME REASON. SO SHE MUST WEAR THE HIJAB. YOU WOULDN'T WANT MEN TO STARE AT YOUR WIFE OR DAUGHTER, WOULD YOU?

THE BURQA IS AFGHAN. IT IS CULTURAL. IT IS NOT MUSLIM. AFGHAN WOMEN WEAR THE BURQA BY THEIR OWN CHOICE.

IF A WOMAN SEES A MAN ONE TIME, SHE MUST NOT LOOK AT HIM A SECOND TIME. ALSO, SHE WILL NOT SEE HIM A SECOND TIME BECAUSE SHE WILL STAY INSIDE.

SURE, OF COURSE A WOMAN SOMETIMES NEEDS TO GET AWAY FROM THINGS, JUST TAKE A WALK. SHE CAN DO THIS WITH HER HUSBAND, OR SISTER, OR AT LEAST HER CHILD.

WHEN A WOMAN GETS OLD, SHE NO LONGER MAKES MEN LUSTFUL. SO SHE DOES NOT HAVE TO WEAR THE BURQA ANYMORE.

"We are not afraid of you," I said.

"Should we be afraid of you?" Steven asked, smiling.

"Of course not!" said the young man.

"Then we are not afraid," said Matt.

There was silence.

Then—

"You must be brave," the young man said, "or crazy!"

"Maybe both!" I said. We raised our teacups.

This time the laughter was equal.

The next morning I ran into the old *mooj* in the toilet. In America even men who are best friends don't always acknowledge one another in the john, so I held back. He gave a little wave; we exchanged salaams and squatted side by side, squirting diarrhea.

"What do American people think of Afghans?" he asked me when we were done wiping off our legs.

"Well," I replied, "it's a huge country. Many different people, many different opinions. But many Americans think Afghans should not kill our soldiers. That they should be grateful for our help."

His eyes twinkled. He wiped his hands on his *shalwar kameez.* "Grateful? Why?"

"For getting rid of the Taliban. And building roads."

"You cannot get rid of the Taliban. They are here. They are Afghans. Do the Taliban look gone to you?" He laughed, pointing at himself. "Listen," he continued, "I have read that George Bush says that we hate you because of your freedoms. But it is not true. We do not hate you. One day, we will drive you out of Afghanistan and govern our own affairs. Peace will come."

"For that to happen," I said, "you will have to kill many Americans."

"Yes," he agreed. "After we kill you, we will welcome you back as tourists and honored guests."

WHERE DID THE MONEY GO?

NINE YEARS LATER, AFGHANISTAN LOOKS MUCH THE SAME: A MESS

AUGUST 29, 2010

Herat, Afghanistan—Okay. The roads are impressive. Specifically, the fact that they exist. When the United States invaded Afghanistan in 2001, more than two decades of civil conflict had left the country bereft of basic infrastructure. Roads, bridges, and tunnels had been bombed and mined. What didn't blow up got ground down by tanks. Maintenance? Don't be funny.

It took them too long to get started, but U.S. occupation forces deserve credit for slapping down asphalt. Brutal, bone-crushing ordeals that used to take four days can be measured in smooth, endless-gray-ribboned hours. Bridges have been replaced. Tunnels have been shored up. Most major highways and major city streets have been paved.

But that's about it.

As of 2008 the United States claimed to have spent $1.3 billion on construction projects in Afghanistan. Where'd it all go? Roads don't cost that much.

That's the Big Question here. As far as anyone can tell, the only sign of economic improvement is a building boomlet: green and pink Arab-style glass-and-marble McMansions, guarded by AK-47-toting guards and owned by politically connected goons, are going up on the outskirts of every Afghan city. Most Afghans still live in squalor that compares unfavorably to places like Mumbai and Karachi. Beggars are everywhere. Most people haven't gotten any help.

"Assistance is coming to Afghanistan, but we don't know how it is spent, where it is spent," Amin Farhang, the Afghan minister of economy, said at the time.

Afghan officials tell a similar story now. "When the Americans came after the eleventh of September, we thought 'good, they will rebuild our country,'" Ghulam Naider Nekpor, commander of Torgundi, a dusty town near the Turkmen border, told me. "Instead of help, they send soldiers. And not only that, they send weapons and money to the other side—Pakistan." (Pakistan's Inter-Services Intelligence agency finances and arms the Taliban.)

"We thought Americans were here to help. Now we see they came to take, and take, and take from us."

There are three big problems.

First: instead of construction, money was wasted on troops. As of 2009—before the Obama surge—the Defense Department had blown through $227 billion in Afghanistan. Bear in mind, the World Bank estimated back in 2002 that the country could have been put on a solid economic footing for about $18 billion.

"Please stop sending soldiers" is a standard plea here. "Can't you send help instead of soldiers?"

The money we wasted on blowing up wedding parties and killing Al Qaeda number twos could have rebuilt Afghanistan twelve times over—or transformed it into a first world country.

As for those soldiers, they aren't doing much. The Taliban range freely over the countryside, raiding and kidnapping at will. The Afghan National Police have ceded most of the country—everything outside the big cities—to the Taliban.

Ninety-nine percent of U.S. troops are either sitting on their butts on military bases surrounded by blast walls and concertina wire or fighting in remote areas along the sparsely populated border with Pakistan. There are supposedly 140,000 U.S. troops here. But most of the country never sees one.

Why aren't Predator drones being used to take out the Taliban bike gangs that rule the countryside and attack motorists? Why don't U.S. troops attack Taliban strongholds in the north, west, and center of Afghanistan? If we're going to spend a quarter of a trillion bucks on troops here, they ought to provide security.

Afghan cops say they know where the bad guys are. But they don't even have the basic tools, like helicopters, needed to go after them. The U.S. military does—but they ignore Afghan requests for help.

Second problem: corruption and American stupidity. They go together; stupid American organizations like USAID pick U.S. contractors or fly-by-night outfits connected to the Karzai regime and fail to audit their expenses. Bills are padded to spectacular extents. Work, when it gets done, is shoddy. Highways paved three years ago are already warped due to inferior roadbeds.

Moreover, work often takes place without consultation with, or the benefit of, locals. No one asks villagers what they want. Outsiders do the work; locals sit and watch. Areas that need a hospital get a road. Those that want a road get a school.

The Frontier Post, a Pakistani newspaper based in the Afghan border towns of Quetta and Peshawar, editorialized: "Afghans have little to be grateful to America for. It may have pumped in billions of dollars in aid—but only theoretically. Practically, much of that has been siphoned off and ploughed back by American contractors, making them rich while Afghans get only lollipops."

Third: the Afghan people are last priority.

In a war for hearts and minds, there's no place for the trickle-down approach. But that's what the United States—when it makes a serious effort, which is rare—does. I wouldn't have invaded Afghanistan in the first place, but if I were put in charge here I would deploy the "trickle-up" approach: direct financial assistance to the people who need it most. Help subsistence farmers buy their own plots of land. Build new houses and apartment blocks for the homeless. Invite bright children to attend colleges and universities tuition-free. Above all, don't let people starve.

We have spent $229 billion here. Meals cost less than a dollar. No Afghan should be starving—yet millions are.

EIGHT: THE BEGINNING OF THE END

We can say with confidence that America will complete its mission in Afghanistan, and achieve our objective of defeating the core of Al Qaeda. Tonight, I can announce that over the next year, another 34,000 American troops will come home from Afghanistan. This drawdown will continue. And by the end of next year, our war in Afghanistan will be over.

—President Barack Obama, February 12, 2013

Yes, of course there will be [areas controlled by the Taliban after the U.S. withdrawal]. And if we were having this conversation ten years from now, I suspect there would (still) be contested areas because the history of Afghanistan suggests that there will always be contested areas.

—General Martin Dempsey, Chairman of the
Joint Chiefs of Staff, April 8, 2013

Once the United States is in your country, they're harder to get rid of than crabs.

The withdrawal date of American troops from Afghanistan has repeatedly been moved back. Now it's 2014—and, to most Americans, it finally looks and feels real.

Well, partially real.

Much like the thousands of military personnel in Okinawa and South Korea two-thirds of a century after the wars there were won,

ANARCHY IS A POLITICAL MOVEMENT THAT ESPOUSES ELIMINATING ALL FORMS OF STATE-BASED GOVERNANCE.

PEOPLE WILL FORM AD HOC COLLECTIVES TO RESOLVE PROBLEMS. I THINK.

NO ONE REALLY KNOWS HOW IT WOULD WORK. BUT THERE'S A CASE STUDY THAT COMES PRETTY CLOSE: AFGHANISTAN, ESPECIALLY IN RURAL DISTRICTS.

Sad little govt. outpost →

PLEASE DON'T KILL US

NO ONE PAVES ROADS. NO ONE BUILDS SCHOOLS. TRASH PILES UP EVERYWHERE. CONTRARY TO THEORY, NO ONE CARES.

Mud bricks for this wall made from dirt pulled from this hole

STRONGMEN TAKE WHAT AND WHOM THEY LIKE, WHENEVER THEY WANT.

THIS HOUSE USED TO BELONG TO THE GOVERNMENT, BUT A COMMANDER TOOK IT.

BUT IT ISN'T ALL BAD:

TRAFFIC MOVES MORE SMOOTHLY WHEN THERE AREN'T LANES OR SIGNALS OR SIGNS.

ALSO, PEOPLE ARE MUCH MORE POLITE IN HEAVILY ARMED SOCIETIES.

VERILY, IT IS A PLEASURE TO MEET YOU, SIR.

NO, NO, THE JOY AND PRIVILEGE ARE MINE.

between ten thousand and fifteen thousand American soldiers, and many more Defense Department–employed mercenaries, will probably remain in Afghanistan until at least 2024. Germany will leave six hundred to eight hundred through 2017 to train Afghan forces. The Obama administration has requested, and the Afghans have agreed, to keep nine military bases scattered throughout the country. The "forever war" is living up to its prescient nickname.

"At first, they said that they are all leaving in 2014, and now every one of them is coming one by one and saying, 'We are not leaving,'" Karzai said in May 2013. It isn't difficult to imagine a scenario—the Karzai regime in danger of being overthrown, for example—that would prompt the U.S. government (or give it an excuse) to reverse course and go back in.

At this writing, however, the situation in Afghanistan remains about the same as I found it in 2010. The neo-Taliban are waiting in the wings, filling vacuums of power created by U.S. and NATO troop withdrawals. Many Afghans, including those who supported the original Taliban movement in 1995 and 1996, are nervously anticipating what comes next.

First: the mineral curse. The oil curse is the tendency of nations with oil or gas reserves to see their economies distorted and their political institutions corrupted. Afghanistan seems poised to suffer the same fate after the (partial) U.S. withdrawal. In June 2010, news broke that Pentagon geologists working with old Soviet-era maps had determined that Afghanistan had an estimated one trillion dollars in untapped mineral reserves. "The previously unknown deposits—including huge veins of iron, copper, cobalt, gold and critical industrial metals like lithium—are so big and include so many minerals that are essential to modern industry that Afghanistan could eventually be transformed into one of the most important mining centers in the world, the United States officials believe," reported *The New York Times*. The gold rush—and lithium rush—are already on, with the China National

Petroleum Corporation and JPMorgan Chase deeply involved in exploitation of Afghan mines. Corruption is endemic. "Not even one afghani has been added to national income from chromite mining," said Laiq Muhammad, the director of mines in Khost. All the loot has been smuggled to Pakistan for the benefit of local warlords.

Second: economic contraction. Everything you see in Afghanistan today—the tacky McMansions in Kabul, the highways, the electrical infrastructure—is financed directly or indirectly through $4 billion a year in foreign aid, the most received by any other nation. A 2011 report by the Senate Committee on Foreign Relations quotes a World Bank estimate that 97 percent of Afghanistan's GDP derives from spending related to the "international military and donor community presence." Among its conclusions: "the unintended consequences of pumping large amounts of money into a war zone cannot be [over]estimated."

Beginning in 2012, the United States slashed its aid budget to $2 billion. "Aid is decreasing very rapidly and markedly," said the International Rescue Committee's country director, Nigel Jenkins. The IRC cut its budget for Afghanistan from $18 million to $9.5 million from 2011 to 2012. "By 2018, the [World Bank] report predicted, 90 percent of that aid [to Afghanistan] will be gone," reported *The New York Times.*

Vanda Felbab-Brown, an Afghanistan specialist at the Brookings Institution, says the windfall has created a mad scrum of corruption, a "contest for the spoils" before the aid bonanza dries up. "The economic system we have created is not a real economy. It's a fake economy," said Mohammad Zafar Salehi of the Afghan women's rights group Young Women for Change.

Small-time crooks in the Karzai regime are trying to steal as much as they can in order to buy tacky houses with pink marble and mirrored windows in the faux Italianate style. Abdul Rashid Dostum, the Uzbek warlord of Mazar, admitted to *Time* in 2009 that he was one of thousands of recipients of the tens of millions of dollars in "ghost

CH·CH·CH·CHANGES

THINGS CHANGE...NOWHERE MORE THAN IN RAPIDLY DEVELOPING/ DISINTEGRATING WARZONES. A PAUCITY OF INFO ONLINE CAUSED ME TO RELY ON MY 2001 EXPERIENCES — MUCH OF WHICH PROVED TO BE HOPELESSLY OUT OF DATE. AMONG THE HIGHLIGHTS:

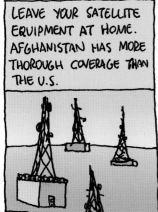

LEAVE YOUR SATELLITE EQUIPMENT AT HOME. AFGHANISTAN HAS MORE THOROUGH COVERAGE THAN THE U.S.

FLY THE FIENDLY SKIES. YOU CAN'T FIND DRIVERS TO TAKE YOU THROUGH RURAL AREAS.

WELCOME TO FLIGHT 3802 FROM MAIMANA TO ZARANJ.

DON'T BLEND IN TOO MUCH. WE GREW BEARDS AND DRESSED LOCAL — AND GOT DETAINED AS TALIBS!

I GREW UP IN DAYTON, IDIOT!

DAYTON, IN KANDAHAR PROVINCE! HA!

THE TALIBAN HAVE EFFECTIVELY BIFURCATED AFGHANISTAN. THIS MADE IT NECESSARY TO ALTER OUR ITINERARY AS FOLLOWS:

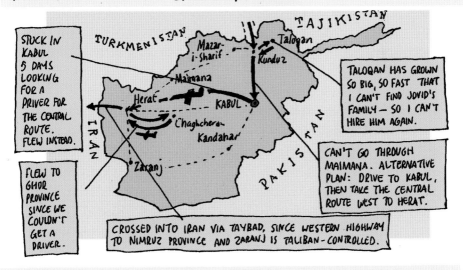

STUCK IN KABUL 5 DAYS LOOKING FOR A DRIVER FOR THE CENTRAL ROUTE. FLEW INSTEAD.

FLEW TO GHOR PROVINCE SINCE WE COULDN'T GET A DRIVER.

TALOQAN HAS GROWN SO BIG, SO FAST THAT I CAN'T FIND JOVID'S FAMILY — SO I CAN'T HIRE HIM AGAIN.

CAN'T GO THROUGH MAIMANA. ALTERNATIVE PLAN: DRIVE TO KABUL, THEN TAKE THE CENTRAL ROUTE WEST TO HERAT.

CROSSED INTO IRAN VIA TAYBAD, SINCE WESTERN HIGHWAY TO NIMRUZ PROVINCE AND ZARANJ IS TALIBAN-CONTROLLED.

TURKMENISTAN · TAJIKISTAN · IRAN · PAKISTAN

Mazar-i-Sharif · Talogan · Kunduz · Maimana · Herat · KABUL · Chaghcheran · Kandahar · Zaranj

AS A FRIEND WROTE ME: "IT'S NOT A GOOD TRIP IF THERE AREN'T SURPRISES."

money"—bags of cash—delivered annually by the CIA to the presidential palace: "I asked for a year up front in cash so that I could build my dream house," Dostum said.

"The biggest source of corruption in Afghanistan," an American official admitted, "was the United States."

The spectacular Kabul Bank scandal, which broke a month after I left Afghanistan, was a case study. According to Kabul Bank founder Sherkhan Farnood, the bank was nothing more than a slush fund for Karzai's cronies, funded by foreign aid. "Depositors put in money, and its owners took it out through fraudulent loans, lining the pockets of a narrow clique tied to President Hamid Karzai and his first vice president, Muhammad Qasim Fahim . . . Mahmood Karzai, the president's brother, had bought a seven percent stake in Kabul Bank with a loan from the bank . . . Haseen Fahim, the first vice president's brother, [stole] millions of dollars deposited by Afghans to finance his own businesses, at least one of which won business from the American-led coalition . . . millions in deposits [were] used to finance President Karzai's re-election campaign the year before," reported *The New York Times*.

Ninety-two percent of Kabul Bank's loan portfolio—$861 million, about five percent of Afghanistan's GDP—went to nineteen people or companies.

No one seems likely to spend a day in prison for these crimes. Or to pay a single afghani of restitution.

Donors will almost certainly withdraw along with the U.S. troop presence, which, if nothing else, provided some semblance of security for the NGO community. "There is the prospect of a lot of white elephants being left behind. That's a really sad prospect," Louise Hancock, head of policy and advocacy for Oxfam in Afghanistan, said in 2013. "People are fed up with Afghanistan. A lot of people are worried they haven't got value for what's been put in."

What happens after the withdrawal, when the international donor community's attention turns elsewhere? "A massive economic constriction" that will further increase economic instability.

Third: civil war. The old dividing lines—Pashtun south versus Tajik-Hazara-Uzbek north, urban vs. rural, Islamist vs. mainline Islam, provincial rivalries—remain. Women are scared that the neo-Taliban would proscribe their participation in civic and outdoor life even more harshly than it is today.

There are new divisions to boot, created by more than a decade of occupation.

"In Afghanistan, if you work with foreigners—not just Americans—they call you an infidel or a spy," an Afghan interpreter for U.S. troops told *The Washington Times*. "Once the Taliban find out that you're working for the U.S. Army, you're done for, and so is your family." Afghans who have cooperated with the Americans and their allies—the Taliban calls them collaborators—are lining up at U.S. embassies and consulates for visas the vast majority of them will probably not receive. Their lives are forfeit.

What happens next? A presidential election is scheduled for April 2014, and although he's changed his mind before, Karzai says he's not running. "[If] we have credible elections, I think we'll be okay for the next five, six years. [If] we don't, there is a real danger that we'll see instability, especially in 2014 as the U.S. troops withdraw," says Saad Mohseni, head of Afghanistan's Tolo Television. But given recent electoral history, which includes numerous districts reporting turnout over one hundred percent, what are the odds of an honest election with results acceptable to most Afghans?

"The Taliban are clever and daring, but they do not seem to have the capability to take over the country again," the BBC World Affairs editor John Simpson wrote in 2012. "A much more likely outcome after 2014 is that the new Afghan government, like the present one, will control only the main cities and the air routes. The rest of the country will be dangerous, and largely in the hands of Taliban groups or warlords. So Afghanistan is not going to turn into Switzerland. But if the outside world keeps its promises about financial help and does not forget about the country again, it could maybe muddle along."

Maybe.

The problem is, the "outside world" doesn't have an awesome record of keeping its commitments. As Afghanistan feels more and more like a bottomless pit of money and lives, the rich countries that have been sustaining the Karzai government will be more likely to respond to domestic concerns that have been neglected since the global economic crisis began in 2008. For example, Greece—which itself stands at the brink of anarchy—decided its seven-million-euro annual budget for maintaining troops in Afghanistan would be better spent at home.

Unrest could spill across the border into neighboring countries. Some analysts worry that Tajikistan and other Central Asian states could become Talibanized. Long-dormant Taliban-trained groups like the Islamic Movement of Uzbekistan, based in Tajikistan but seeking to overthrow the U.S.-backed dictatorship of Uzbek president Islam Karimov, recently reconstituted itself as the Islamic Jihad Union in preparation for the coming power vacuum left by withdrawing NATO forces.

"Mounting discontent and social tensions in Tajikistan will make an ideal hideout for the Taliban and al Qa'eda elements," states Nirmala Joshi's "Reconnecting India and Central Asia," a 2010 report for the Central Asia–Caucasus Institute and Silk Road Studies Program. And China frets over the Turkestan Islamic Party (TIP), a Xinjiang-based Uyghur group that seeks to reestablish an independent Muslim state in China's Far West. "Concerns about Islamist militancy on its western border have only heightened since the Uyghur riots of July 2009 and are likely to increase as the United States withdraws," Christian

Le Mière, then editor of *Jane's Intelligence Review*, wrote in *Foreign Affairs*. "As the United States begins its military withdrawal and drone strikes become less frequent, China worries that the TIP will gain greater freedom of movement."

This could provoke a new New Great Game, or even a New Cold War. "As Washington shows its impatience with the Karzai regime . . . Kabul is beginning to look for new supporters and patrons," Le Mière remarked.

Russia is worried enough about the Taliban that its leaders are considering stepping up support for Karzai. Russian interior minister Anatoly Kulikov told military officers in 2013 that "real power on the ground belongs to the Taliban" after the International Security Assistance Force pulls out.

Le Mière says Karzai is being pulled into Beijing's orbit. "As the regional hegemon, China is the obvious choice. The interest appears to be mutual." Were China, Russia—or Iran, which enjoys historical and cultural ties, because Afghanistan was once part of the Persian Empire—to become more influential in Afghanistan and Central Asia, which has the world's largest untapped energy reserves, the United States would likely get involved again.

Even the neo-Taliban are worried.

Muhammad, a local Taliban commander in southern Zabul province, told *The Daily Beast* that in response to the "popular uprising" of Afghan National Army troops and local militia financed by U.S. Special Forces they would be deploying suicide bombers as part of a summer 2013 offensive.

"Things are really mixed up," said Muhammad. "Our fighters are not clear about who to kill and who not to kill. Tribals and Punjabis [Pakistanis] are coming in higher numbers than ever this year." The trouble is, they operate autonomously, not under Taliban command. "Before, these Pakistanis were scattered among our Afghan fighters.

Chaghcheran, Ghor province

Now they are coming in organized groups with their own command."
Pakistani's Inter-Services Intelligence agency, an old player in Afghanistan, was funding and training the newcomers. They're dangerous
and indiscriminate. "They came here for jihad with their blood boiling
and they want to kill."

In the South, particularly around Kandahar, where the Taliban have
always been popular, people are looking forward to the withdrawal of
NATO troops as an opportunity to see peace restored and their hard-
line Pashtunized brand of political Islam prevail. In Kabul and other
urban areas, including Mazar-i-Sharif, there is a feeling of heightened
tension, of imminent doom. A certain order has prevailed for thirteen
years, and the protectors of that order—corrupt and violent and inept
as they may be—are about to leave, with little concern for the people
who became dependent upon the new society that they helped create.
They have cellphones and they have houses—at least some of them
have houses—and they have cars—well, some of them have cars—and

they can go to the movies and they can listen to music, but they are terrified.

WE HAVE FOUND THE BAD APPLE—AND HE IS US
FEBRUARY 21, 2012

Staff Sergeant Robert Bales is accused of going on a shooting spree on March 11, 2012, that left sixteen civilians dead in southeastern Afghanistan. As the New York *Daily News* put it: "The killings sparked protests in Afghanistan, endangered relations between the two countries and threatened to upend American policy over the decade-old war."

Why the fuss? This is nothing new. Not to the Afghans.

Over the last ten years, U.S. forces have been slaughtering Afghan civilians like they were going out of style. There have been countless massacres of supposed "insurgents" or "terrorists." Who invariably turned out to have been ordinary men, women, and children going about their daily routines.

The only difference between the Bales massacre and other acts of bloodshed is that he acted on a freelance basis, without orders from his commanding officer. Bales's actions were so similar to the "normal" behavior of U.S. soldiers that Afghan witnesses weren't surprised.

Atrocities are business as usual. Afghans have learned that their lives are cheap—not to them, but to the young men and women who patrol their streets and man explosives-laden drones from the other side of the world.

On July 7, 2012, for example, an air strike in Khost province killed at least thirteen civilians, mostly women and children. On December 19, 2011, U.S. occupation troops and Afghan collaborators conducting a "night raid" on the home of an antinarcotics official in Paktia province shot and killed his pregnant wife. At least eight children died in a February 9, 2012, air strike in Kapisa province. A helicopter gunship opened fire on a school in Nangahar province on February 22, 2012, injuring nine girls.

I don't have enough space to provide a complete accounting of recent U.S. atrocities in occupied Afghanistan, but here's a taste: U.S. Special Forces operatives alone admit killing over one thousand five hundred Afghan civilians just in night raids during ten months in 2010 and early 2011.

Afghans know the deal.

Americans don't.

It's intentional. The U.S. government doesn't want ordinary American citizens to know how their "heroic" soldiers behave in remote combat zones. America's cult of militarism, so important to the congressmen whose careers depend on defense contractor contributors and to the media outlets for whom war means higher ratings, requires a placid, compliant populace lulled into the ridiculous belief that the U.S. military is defending freedom.

Sergeant Bales is a PR problem. His decision to blow away women and children for no reason whatsoever belies the hero-troops narrative. It's too icky for even a "support our troops"–besotted public to ignore. So Sergeant Bales has become a political football.

Shortly after the suspect turned himself in, the Army spin machine revved up.

"When it all comes out, it will be a combination of stress, alcohol and domestic issues—he just snapped," an unnamed "senior government official" told *The New York Times*. Just one of those things. What can you do?

Pointing to the fact that Bales's spree took place while he was on his fourth tour of duty, his lawyer is laying the groundwork for a

PTSD defense. "We all know what's going on over there [in Afghanistan], but you don't really know it until you listen to somebody like him," John Henry Browne said to reporters. In other words: War makes people nuts. Blame war, not my client.

After incidents like this, one can always count upon the political class to unleash the "one bad apple" chestnut.

"This incident is tragic and shocking, and does not represent the exceptional character of our military and the respect that the United States has for the people of Afghanistan," President Obama read from a prepared statement. "Obviously what happened this weekend," he added in a Denver TV interview, "was absolutely tragic and heartbreaking, but when you look at what hundreds of thousands of our military personnel have achieved under enormous strain, you can't help but be proud generally, and I think it's important for us to make sure we are not in Afghanistan longer than we need to be."

Don't blame the war, says Obama. Don't blame the troops. Whether they're shooting up their high school or their post office, some people go nuts sometimes. Can't be helped.

Of course, from the Afghan point of view, this is low-grade, elementary-school-level spin.

Afghans don't wonder whether the former All-American footballer from Norwood, Ohio, was driven crazy by combat, was like that all along, or if this is another Jessica Lynch / Pat Tillman Pentagon lie that will wind up as something completely different from what we're being told now.

Afghans don't care why.

The way the Afghans see it is straightforward. The United States invaded their country. Without just cause. The United States has imposed a ruthless and cruel occupation that has left tens of thousands of their countrymen dead or seriously wounded. The United States has installed and propped up Hamid Karzai's corrupt puppet regime in Kabul.

To the Afghans, Sergeant Bales didn't kill those sixteen people in Kandahar province. The United States did. Obama did. We did. After all, if we hadn't invaded and occupied Afghanistan, Bales wouldn't have been there in the first place.

Reporters are digging up dirt on Sergeant Bales's marriage and supposed drinking problems in order to distract us from this simple fact.

FROM 2001 TO 2005, THE AMERICAN PEOPLE WERE ALL FOR THE WAR IN AFGHANISTAN.

IF WE **LEAVE**, WOMEN WILL BE BACK IN **BURQAS** AND GETTING **STONED**

BUT THAT'S HAPPENING **NOW**

IT CAME FROM KABUL: THE 9-11 STORY

I KEPT SCREAMING THAT IT WAS WRONG & UNWINNABLE.

PARTLY BECAUSE OF OPPONENTS LIKE ME, THE AMERICAN PEOPLE HAVE CHANGED THEIR MINDS. NOW MOST THINK IT WAS A TERRIBLE MISTAKE. THEY WANT OUT.

FROM 2006 TO 2010, HOWEVER, THE U.S. ACTUALLY, FINALLY, BELATEDLY, SLIGHTLY HELPED AFGHANISTAN REBUILD.

WE CALL THIS "CONSTRUCTION EQUIPMENT." THEY USE IT TO SPREAD "PAVEMENT."

Kom

BUT YOU ONLY GET ONE CHANCE TO MAKE A GOOD FIRST IMPRESSION. WE'RE LIKE AN ABUSIVE SPOUSE WHO FINALLY GETS SOBER AND STARTS ACTING DECENT.

THEY'RE JUST NOT INTO US ANYMORE.

(IF THEY EVER WERE)

NINE: THE ONLY WAY TO WIN

The enemy hopes they can hide until we tire. But we're going to prove them wrong. We will never tire.
> —George W. Bush, November 22, 2001

"My goal is to make sure that by 2014 we have transitioned, Afghans are in the lead, and it is a goal to make sure we are not still engaged in combat operations of the sort we are involved in now," Obama told a news conference. He said the United States endorsed NATO's plan to transfer security responsibility to Afghan security forces by 2014, but stressed that counter-terrorism operations against Al Qaeda in the region would likely continue after that date.
> —Reuters, November 20, 2010

Percent of Americans in favor of the war:

2001: 88 percent
2010: 35 percent
2013: 17 percent

Why does America keep getting sucked into foreign quagmires? Conservatives blame good intentions gone wrong along with a lack of resolve. Liberals point to ignorance and naïveté about places we don't know enough about. Progressive critics of U.S. foreign policy don't think we get sucked in at all, that the politics of disruption are at the core of an aggressive form of neocolonialism, the quest not for old-fashioned empire but postmodern open markets ripe for exploitation by international corporations. Word count reveals where I stand.

Whatever your politics there is no denying history: beginning with Thomas Jefferson's dispatch of marines to Tripoli during the Barbary Wars of the early 1800s, the United States has been engaged in aggressive wars against foreign states virtually without interruption. Afghanistan is merely one of the most recent.

Afghanistan is notable, not only as America's longest war, but also as one that sneaked up on us. True, the British didn't feel much to worry about in 1839, nor the Russians in 1979. Both those disasters began as routs; the Afghans melted into the mountains and the occupation was a relatively calm affair. Things degenerated slowly but inevitably. In an age of instantaneous mass media and communication, the fact that Americans were lulled into complacency by early 2002 yet worried sick by 2010 is something of a surprise and an accomplishment on the part of the Afghan resistance.

The danger of America's experience in Afghanistan is that ordinary American citizens will believe their politicians and military leaders when they assert that there are lessons to be learned and that they will learn them. Andrey Avetisyan, Russia's ambassador to Afghanistan in Kabul, argues that the United States and its NATO allies ought to have spent more time and money building than bombing. "All important infrastructure or industrial projects here [in Afghanistan] were fulfilled by the Soviet Union. The fact is that not a single big project—infrastructure, industrial or agriculture—has been implemented during the past nine years . . . a school here, a hospital there, some small roads, but nothing big. I think the biggest mistake has been focusing on military efforts."

Avetisyan's immediate predecessor had personal experience in Afghanistan, having worked as a press attaché and KGB agent in Kabul during the Soviet occupation. In 2008 he confided his frustration with U.S.-led forces whose leaders he had tried to engage: "Because we deployed very easily into the major cities, we didn't give much thought to what was happening in the countryside," where the stirrings of opposition that grew into a full-fledged insurgency began, he told *The New York Times*. "One of our mistakes was staying, instead of leaving. After we changed the regime, we should have handed over and said goodbye. But we didn't. And the Americans haven't, either."

"They listen, but they do not hear," he said with another wry smile. "Their attitude is, 'The past is the past,' and that they know more than I do."

Others say the occupation soldiers are imperious, arrogant, and cruel. "The behavior of Red Army troops [was] much better than what we see from the American-NATO forces," says Faheem Dashty, editor of the *Kabul Weekly* newspaper. Whether the Russians were really nicer, or they're benefiting from fading memories of their occupation, this is something you hear from a lot of Afghans.

And of course there are the civilian casualties. If only the United States stopped blowing up wedding parties and random women and children from remote-operated drone planes, the Monday morning quarterbacks assert, they would be popular.

Lessons learned from the wars of the past, we tell ourselves, will help us win the wars of the future. Nothing is farther from the truth. The way to win wars is not to fight them in the first place—optional wars, anyway. Though tinted differently than those of Vietnam and Iraq, the lessons of Afghanistan are at core exactly the same. Invading other countries, whether to steal their land or poach their natural resources or pressure their neighbors or exert regional influence, is an enterprise with a cost-to-benefit ratio that simply doesn't work. Supply lines are too long. When it costs a million dollars to keep a soldier in the field for a year, the expenses are too high. There may be profits to be made. But they will be erased, and then some.

When will the United States understand that it cannot afford optional wars, those of aggression? Only, I fear, when its economy collapses to the point that its political class can no longer borrow to wage them. That day draws nearer—in no small part because of the unaffordable price of wars like the one we're losing in Afghanistan.

AN HOUR FLIGHT ON A SOVIET-MADE YAK-10 "TAJIK AIR" PLANE RENTED TO KAM AIR, FROM GHOR PROVINCE BACK TO HERAT

A NIGHT INSIDE THE HEAVILY FORTIFIED HOTEL NAZARY IN HERAT

A HIGH-SPEED TWO-HOUR DRIVE FROM HERAT THROUGH WESTERN HERAT PROVINCE, SUPPOSEDLY CONTROLLED BY TALIBS (LOOKED LOW-KEY ENOUGH)

THEN: THE BORDER.

Baggage handler kid. Agreed to 50 afghanis. We gave him 90. He yelled for more.

ARE YOU **KIDDING**?

YOU MUST BE TED, MATT, AND STEVEN.

Our Iranian fixer

ALI?

Passport Control

YOU KNOW, YOU ARE THE FIRST AMERICANS TO ENTER IRAN FROM AFGHANISTAN. AT LEAST IN 15 YEARS. SO IRANIAN INTELLIGENCE NEEDS TO FINGERPRINT AND INTERVIEW YOU.

NO ONE KNOWS WHAT TO MAKE OF US.

NOTES

Prologue: The End of the Beginning

21 *Mullah Mohammed Omar*: "U.S. Faces 'Absolute Defeat,' Taliban Leader Purportedly Says," CNN, November 25, 2009, available at www.cnn.com/2009/WORLD/asiapcf/11/25/afghanistan.taliban/index.html#cnnSTCText.

22 *"Over cups of tea and biscuits"*: Tony Karon, "What They're Saying About the War," *Time*, November 23, 2001, available at www.time.com/time/nation/article/0,8599,185637,00.html.

36 *at least twenty-two thousand bombs*: Anthony H. Cordesman, "The Lessons of Afghanistan: Warfighting, Intelligence, Force Transformation, Counterproliferation, and Arms Control," Center for Strategic and International Studies, available at http://docs.google.com/viewer?a=v&q=cache:3zQFO3MQOIsJ:defbib.kma.nl/art2/pdf/ada/lessonsofafghan.pdf+total+ordnance+dropped+on+afghanistan&hl=en&gl=us&pid=bl&srcid=ADGEESgFOPVFbR5DHYWr3-oSQLOOYrwSwYyXLmuiZvhMLkAx9pwdkKB1BhpII_-cDmADNbmyX0-NA2FZfP7MewSdiClb2mc7bps0cQhIjNwWee1m3eiQBbQGCvBbaC2nk7s4qRrXD_eJ&sig=AHIEtbRc5uYpr5xUaJqmRQvdPRI9-yFa8A.

36 *thousands of "cluster bombs"*: Fernando Termentini, "From Kosovo to Afghanistan, Cluster Bombs Again," *Journal of Mine Action*, no 7.2 (2003), available at http://maic.jmu.edu/JOURNAL/7.2/focus/fernando/fernando.htm.

36 *Each CBU-87*: Marc W. Herold, "Above the Law and Below Morality: Data on 11 Weeks of US Cluster-Bombing of Afghanistan," *Cursor*, February 1, 2002, available at www.rawa.org/cluster2.htm.

1. The Beginning of the End

41   *Zamir Kabulov*: "Russia's Ambassador in Kabul on Fighting the Taliban: Don't Bother with More Troops . . . That Will Just Make It Worse," *Daily Mail*, Mail Online edition, September 13, 2009, available at www.dailymail.co.uk/news /worldnews/article-1212960/Russias-ambassador-Kabul-fighting-Taliban-Dont -bother-troops--just-make-worse.html.

41   *"the wrong war"*: Teddy Davis, "Wrong Way or Wrong War?" ABC News, September 6, 2004, available at http://abcnews.go.com/Politics/story?id=120221& page=1.

41   *"Let me be clear"*: Kevin Hechtkopf, "Text: Obama's Plan for Afghanistan and Pakistan," CBS News, March 27, 2009, available at www.cbsnews.com/8301 -503544_162-4896758-503544.html.

42   *So Obama set a deadline*: David E. Sanger and Peter Baker, "Afghanistan Drawdown to Begin in 2011, Officials Say," *New York Times*, sec. Asia Pacific, December 1, 2009, available at www.nytimes.com/2009/12/02/world/asia/02policy .html.

2. Return of the War Tourist

81   *"Travelers are under the ongoing threat"*: Sophia Banay, "Most Dangerous Destinations 2006," *Forbes*, February 16, 2006, available at www.forbes.com/2006 /02/16/dangerous-travel-destinations-cx_sb_0216feat_ls.html?partner=links.

93   *a suicide bomber rammed his car*: Bill Roggio, "Taliban Suicide Bomber Strikes Afghan Police in Kunduz," *The Long War Journal*, August 5, 2010, available at www.longwarjournal.org/archives/2010/08/taliban_suicide_bomb_14.php.

93   *Nader Nadery*: Rod Nordland, "In Bold Display, Taliban Order Stoning Deaths," *New York Times*, sec. Asia Pacific, August 16, 2010, available at www .nytimes.com/2010/08/17/world/asia/17stoning.html.

95   *gift roads*: Matthew J. Nasuti, "The Ring Road: A Gift Afghanistan Cannot Afford," KabulPress.org, September 29, 2009, available at www.kabulpress.org/my /spip.php?article4093.

97   *one-in-four chance*: "25 Most Dangerous Neighborhoods," *Daily Finance*, 2012, available at www.walletpop.com/photos/most-dangerous-neighborhoods.

4. The Second Battle of Kunduz

121 *Abdul Wahed Omarkhiel*: Keith B. Richburg, "As Taliban Makes Comeback in Kunduz Province, War Spreads to Northern Afghanistan," *Washington Post*, sec. Asia/Pacific, March 19, 2010, available at www.washingtonpost.com/wp-dyn /content/article/2010/03/18/AR2010031805399.html.

123 *a thousand motorbikes*: Adam Entous and Alister Bull, "Pakistan Secretly Backed Taliban: Wikileaks," Reuters, U.S. edition, July 25, 2010, available at www.reuters .com/article/2010/07/26/idUSN25163580.

124 *Joshua Partlow*: Joshua Partlow, "Taliban Takes Hold in Once-Peaceful Northern Afghanistan," *Washington Post*, sec. Asia/Pacific, August 15, 2010, available at www.washingtonpost.com/wp-dyn/content/article/2010/08/14/AR2010081 402317.html.

5. Kabul, City of Blast Walls

145 *"If you're thinking about"*: Dion Nissenbaum, "Yoga, Blast Walls and Life in the Afghan 'Kabubble,'" McClatchyDC, July 15, 2010, available at www.mcclatchydc .com/2010/07/15/97594/yoga-blast-walls-and-life-in-the.html.

6. Coming April 2067: The Trans-Afghanistan Pipeline

171 *"About 735 kilometers"*: "Pakistan Seeks U.S. Security for Gas Pipeline," *Wall Street Journal*, January 28, 2011, available at http://online.wsj.com/news/articles /SB10001424052748703956604576109282747371782.

7. Sleeping with the Taliban

179 *"Afghans (including the Taliban)"*: Robert Young Pelton, "Afghanistan: Obama's Speech" (online forum message), Black Flag Cafe, December 2, 2009, available at http://cafe.comebackalive.com/viewtopic.php?f=1&t=46581.

179 *Sayed Muhammad Gulabzoi*: Ivan Watson, "Experts: Lessons of Soviets in Afghanistan Ignored," NPR, *All Things Considered*, June 6, 2008, available at www .npr.org/templates/story/story.php?storyId=91240615.

8. The Beginning of the End

199 *"We can say with confidence"*: "Obama Says 34,000 US Troops to Leave Afghanistan," Dawn.com, February 13, 2013.

201 *"At first, they said that they are all leaving"*: Matthew Rosenberg, "Karzai Says U.S. Bases Can Stay, Raising Some Eyebrows in the West," *New York Times*, sec. Asia Pacific, May 9, 2013, available at www.nytimes.com/2013/05/10/world /asia/karzai-says-us-can-keep-afghan-bases-after-2014.html.

206 *"Mounting discontent and social tensions"*: Nirmala Joshi (ed.), "Reconnecting India and Central Asia: Emerging Security and Economic Dimensions," executive summary, Central Asia–Caucasus Institute and Silk Road Studies Program, 2010, available at www.silkroadstudies.org/new/inside/publications/Joshi.html.

9. The Only Way to Win

215 *"The enemy hopes they can hide"*: Brian Knowlton, "Exit for Foreigners Studied as Deadline Nears for Taliban," *New York Times*, November 22, 2001, available at www.nytimes.com/2001/11/22/news/22iht-attack_ed3__22.html

215 *"My goal is to make sure"*: Ross Colvin and Matt Spetalnick, "Obama Sees End to Afghan Combat Mission by the End of 2014," Reuters, U.S. edition, November 20, 2010, available at www.reuters.com/article/2010/11/20/us-nato-summit -usa-idUSTRE6AJ10820101120.

215 *2001: 88 percent*: Karlyn Bowman, "America and the War on Terror," American Enterprise Institute, July 24, 2008, available at www.aei.org/paper/22819.

215 *2010: 35 percent*: Amanda Terkel, "63 Percent of Americans Oppose War in Afghanistan," *Huffington Post*, U.S. edition, December 30, 2010, available at www .huffingtonpost.com/2010/12/30/63-percent-of-american-public-opposes-war -afghanistan_n_802765.html.

215 *2013: 17 percent*: Maya Rhodan, "Support for Afghanistan War Hits New Low," *Time*, Swampland blog, December 30, 2013, available at http://swampland.time .com/2013/12/30/support-for-afghanistan-war-hits-new-low.

217 *"The behavior of Red Army troops"*: "US Troops Pass Soviets' Afghan Stay," Al Jazeera, English edition, sec. Central and South Asia, November 27, 2010, available at http://english.aljazeera.net/news/asia/2010/11/2010112711249788109.html.

ACKNOWLEDGMENTS

Unless you're writing in prison, writing a book is a collaborative effort. Even then, someone has to sneak out your manuscript.

First I must thank the numerous Afghans who gave me their hospitality, protection, and guidance during my visits to their country, not infrequently risking their lives to help me. Due to what is euphemistically termed "the security situation," it would be reckless to name my Afghan friends here. Afghanistan is a place where friendships are hard to come by and last a lifetime when you find them; I know I'll struggle to achieve the Afghans' high standard of loyalty in my remaining years.

My traveling companions during the two journeys chronicled in this book, in 2001 and 2010, made the difference between life and death in a place where snap judgments mean everything. In 2001 I entered the warzone with two intrepid women, my wife, Judy, and my Hollywood agent, Mary Anne Patey. Two respected colleagues and friends, the cartoonists Matt Bors and Steven L. Cloud, were a pleasure to explore the nation with.

My friend and cartoonist colleague Stephanie McMillan served as a faithful and diligent digital lifeline in 2010, tracking our movements, providing logistical updates, and, not least, downloading my satellite transmissions, coloring the daily cartoon blogs, and disseminating them electronically.

My literary agent, Sandy Dijkstra, patiently and intelligently moved the idea for this book through several iterations. Also at the Sandra Dijkstra Literary Agency, thanks are due to Elise Capron, Andrea Cavallaro, Roz Foster, and Thao Le.

At Hill and Wang / Farrar, Straus and Giroux, Thomas LeBien developed my idea into a format he could sign up and provided support for my 2010 trip to Afghanistan, including equipment. Executive Editor Sean McDonald was a fantastic, patient sounding board and a methodical, smart shepherd who improved my voice. Taylor Sperry's superb line edits saw the forest for the dead trees. Abby Kagan did the interior design. I love Adly Elewa's cover. Thanks also to Debra Helfand and Mareike Grover, who handled copy and production.

To my family and friends: thank you for worrying about me.

A NOTE ABOUT THE AUTHOR

Ted Rall is the author and illustrator of many graphic novels and books of political criticism and travel writing, including *To Afghanistan and Back: A Graphic Travelogue*, *Silk Road to Ruin: Is Central Asia the New Middle East?*, *The Year of Loving Dangerously*, and *The Book of Obama: From Hope and Change to the Age of Revolt*. He lives in East Hampton, New York.